Jean Ritchie's
dulcimer people

Oak Publications, New York
Music Sales Limited, London

Cover photograph, and photographs of Jean Ritchie and her
family were taken by George Pickow. Other photographs were
supplied by individual artists and craftsmen.

Book design by Iris Weinstein

Music Sales Limited, 78 Newman Street, W1 London

Music Sales (Pty) Limited
27 Clarendon Street, Artarmon, Sydney NSW, Australia

International Standard Book Number 0-8256-0142-8
Library of Congress Card Catalog Number 73-77716

Contents

This is the "holler". Walking up the mountain road beyond the Ritchie home (near the mouth of the Elkhorn Branch), we take the right hand fork of Elkhorn, always pausing to rest a minute at this place to enjoy the view of the left hand fork, for we can see clear to the head of the holler. Today, this view is marred by strip mining, but is still beautiful.

The Family Dulcimer Goes From Home To The Beyond: A Very Personal History

My father, Balis Ritchie, showed me how to play the old black dulcimer when I was big enough not to break it, when I was about five or six years old (1927 or so), here in our home in the mountains of Eastern Kentucky. Before that, I'd slip it down, hide behind the davenport and play any old way, and he never knew about that, since he was hard of hearing and the dulcimer is soft-toned. I had pretty much taught myself when one rainy afternoon he undertook to teach me, saying, as we sat down on the porch, "Well, if you can play, you can play, and if you can't, you can't!" When I began to play for him, just the way I used to fool around behind his back, he listened in surprise and then said he reckoned I was a natural-born musician.

Our dulcimer was made by J. Edward Thomas, who used to travel about with a cart up and down the hollers, selling dulcimers. He was from Bath, Kentucky, and was the first person around there to make the instrument, that anybody can remember. Uncle Will Singleton, across the swinging bridge at Viper (our village), and our distant cousin Jethro Amburgy, over a few hills in Hindman, Knott County, both built from patterns given them by Thomas, although Uncle Will didn't usually put a double curve in his sound boxes. If the instrument had three strings, it was called a dulcimer; if it had four strings, it was called a harmony (har mō′ny), but most of them were three-stringed. Uncle Will made only three-stringers, and an occasional "courtin' dulcimer," one sound-box which had two fretboards, built to be played by two people facing each other.

Folks around here played only in the old simple way, as described in my first book about this instrument, *The Dulcimer Book* (Oak Publications). I think that this was because we were still not instrument-minded; we were just begin-ning to venture beyond the unaccompanied-ballad stage. The song and the story it told were the important things; the accompaniment, if any, was simple and secondary. I cannot remember any outstanding instrumentalists from those days, but remember scores of *great* singers.

How the picture has changed! When I first began traveling about the country, going before city audiences with our traditional songs and playing the dulcimer, I found only two other people doing anything similar: John Jacob Niles, who lived near Louisville, Kentucky, and Andrew Rowen Summers of Abingdon, Virginia (of course there were others—Dr. Patrick Gainer in West Virginia and the I. G. Greers in North Carolina, but I did not know of them at that time).

Our family had known Mr. Niles from the time I was about ten years old. One day my sister Mallie looked out the door and threw up her hands, "Lordie mercy, look what's coming up the branch!" It was young John Niles carrying Miss Doris Ulmann, a photographer, piggy-back up the holler so she wouldn't have to wade in the mud puddles. When they got to our place, he set her down and she asked if she might take our pictures as we went about our work. She did, taking Mom Ritchie at the loom, the spinning wheel and the soap-kettle; Dad playing his dulcimer; me with my dolls and pretties; and all of us singing on our front steps. Mr. Niles asked us to sing for him, and took the words down, and told us that on the way up to our house he had seen a dulcimer like ours hanging on the wall at Homeplace, the rural community center at Ary. Friends at Homeplace later told us that this was the first dulcimer Mr. Niles had ever seen. This must have been about 1930 or 1931, and a short time later he began making and playing his own "concert dulcimers," larger and more ornate than the ones he had seen.

They soon became the center of interest at his public appearances. Our paths have crossed several times since that first meeting, and we have shared the concert stage. John Jacob Niles has made many record albums and received honors throughout the world for his singing and his compositions. Now in his eighties, he is still composing, singing and playing the dulcimer.

Andrew Rowen Summers, born in 1912, was a sweet-voiced tenor who sang old ballads and hymns to beautiful, precisely-set dulcimer arrangements. Although he was a lawyer, he had sung and collected the folk songs of Virginia for many years. He was singing at one of the White Top Festivals in the 1940s when he saw his first dulcimer being played by an old man past eighty. That same dulcimer was willed to him two years later, and he used it in his folk song recitals until his death at the close of the 1960s. He was well-known and loved in Virginia and surrounding states and in New York where he lived for awhile and worked as a very successful designer of furniture. He recorded several albums of his Virginia songs for Folkways Records (see discography). We met for the first time in New York in 1950, backstage at the McMillin Theater at Columbia University, and for the last time as participants at the Berkeley Festival in California, 1964.

Andrew Rowen Summers, second from left.

I was born in 1922, the baby in our large family of fourteen. I began performing in a small way while I was growing up at home, at community programs in our two-room schoolhouse in Viper, at 4-H Club meetings, and at the County

Fair in Hazard, our county seat. My Dad called that, "singing for *people*," as opposed to singing for oneself, I suppose, which is what folks generally did, especially those who played dulcimers. At Cumberland College, Williamsburg, Kentucky, and later at the University of Kentucky, Lexington, the thing to do was to sing in the glee club and the choirs, take voice and piano lessons, and try to imitate opera stars; so, for a brief period, the dulcimer sat on the fireboard at home, played only by Dad and strummed a little by some of the other family members.

Then came the day when I was home from college. I was going around the house singing, *Barbry Ellen*, in the new voice I had been working on at school. Dad looked up from his paper and said, "What's all that screeching about? Somebody a-hurting you?" I had to admit that *Barbry Ellen* did sound pretty ridiculous sung fancy like that, and I never took another voice lesson.

During World War II, I was drafted, more or less, to teach school. My first school turned out to be a one-teacher school of some thirty-one students, primer class through eighth grade, at the head of Little Leatherwood Creek. That holler was five miles long, a narrow dirt road that was often the same thing as the creek bed. Each Friday evening after walking out to the mouth of the holler, I waited for the shaky old bus to take me on the new highway that followed the curves of the river down to Viper and home. During the week I took room and board with Mr. and Mrs. Mae Halcomb, "Big Mae," and "Aunt Jude," distant kinsmen of ours. In the little schoolhouse and on the playground, the old music came out for me again, stronger than ever. I sang Ritchie songs for the children and they sang theirs for me. We went for long picnic-ambles in the hills, and waded the branches observing minnows, crawdads, grampuses and other water-life—all kinds of frogs and snakes in the waters and on the land. We had long recesses and dinner-time singing-game sessions on the hard-packed earth of the playground. We learned precious little from books that year, but what a beautiful world it was!

When finally I was graduated from the University as a social work major in June of 1946, Professor Harold Wetzel, my advisor and teacher and the head of the new department (Social work was just getting started and I had been the first student to sign up for that new department!) called me in and told me that there was a job for me in New York if I wanted it, as a group worker at the Henry Street Settlement. We decided that, since "relief" was the only organized social work program existing in eastern Kentucky, it could do me no harm to work in New York for awhile, gaining knowledge of their programs. That is how it came about that, about the middle of June, 1947, I took up residence with some twenty others in the settlement "family" at 301 Henry Street. Helen Hall Kellog was the director then; Ralph and Ruth Tefferteller were in charge of the programs. They started off my new career with a roomful of lively eight-nine-ten-year-olds for after-school games and songs. My co-worker was Bill Pressman, who sang folk songs, played country-style guitar, had a wonderful gentle way with the children, and without whose help I certainly would never have survived that baptism of fire (the Settlement was in an extremely permissive stage just then, and I was fresh from an upbringing that had stressed obedience, respect for elders, etc.).

Again, my heritage came to aid me—the family games, songs, the dulcimer. The children called me "Kentucky," and one little girl grew so fond of me that she cried when she found that I wasn't Jewish. They had such exotic folklore—so different from anything in my background, and they in turn never tired of hearing about my own childhood and growing up in the mountains, our customs, songs, ways of work and play. Other settlement workers and visiting teachers, passing by our room, would hear the dulcimer music, and later they would ask me to a party or to visit their school classes. . . . "and to be sure to bring your music!"

My first attempt at playing before a formal New York audience was on November 22, 1947, at a New York University Alumni Tea. Bill Pressman went along to bolster my courage, and we sang a duet or two. The songs included *Lazy John, My Pretty Little Pink,* and *Black is the Color of My Truelove's Hair.* As I recollect, they liked the songs well enough, but they were *thrilled* with the dulcimer.

In April of the following year, the Educational Alliance, a settlement house around the corner from Henry Street, ran a folksong concert and the worker there, Bernie Klayman, asked me to sing. At that event, a young man came onstage wearing a British army coat, and removed one shoe so that he could pat his foot on the microphone. He was introduced as Oscar Brand, Shoeless Troubador from Canada. When it came my turn to sing, the

microphone could not move low enough to pick up the dulcimer's soft tones, so Oscar held the microphone at the right level until someone came up with the idea of placing a contact microphone on my lap, underneath the instrument. I think that was the first electrified dulcimer.

That spring too, a little later, I met Alan Lomax, then working at Decca Records. He recorded many Ritchie songs from me, for the Library of Congress, and asked me to sing at an evening he was running for Columbia University, the Fourth Annual Festival of Contemporary Music Folksong Evening, at the McMillin Theater. Our evening, May 15th at 8:30, was billed as, "Ballads, Hoe-Downs, Spirituals and Blues—played and sung by Mrs. Texas Gladden, Virginia ballad singer; Hobart Smith, Virginia Mountain fiddler; Jean Ritchie, Kentucky Mountain Dulcimer Player; Brownie Maghee, North Carolina blues-guitarist; Vera Hall, Alabama spiritual singer; Dan Burleigh, blues pianist; Peter Seeger, topical ballad singer; Alan Lomax, narrator." While we were backstage getting acquainted, a small wiry man with curly hair standing on end, came bounding into the room, waving a guitar and blowing into all the microphones. Alan and Peter Seeger knew him, all clapping each other on the back and laughing, then the man looked at us and scratched his head and grinned, "This is just ole Woody, come to wish you luck!" The rest of us thought he was pretty strange. He didn't stay for the program, and it was not until a few days later, on May 20, to be exact, that Woody

Woody Guthrie at WNYC. He showed me some chords on the guitar.

Guthrie and I heard each other's music for the first time. This was at the "Spring Fever Hootenanny," at Irving Plaza in New York City, run by People's Songs, and besides Woody and I there were The Weavers, Betty Sanders, Oscar Brand and Ernie Leiberman. After the program, we were all congratulating one another, and Woody ran over to examine the dulcimer, exclaiming, "Hey, what do you call that contraption? Why, you can get more music out of them three strings than I can out of twelve!" One of the others said, "There goes Woody Guthrie, always the ladies' man!"

As time passed, my dulcimer began to be a familiar sight around the New York folk scene. I had no case for the instrument, and carried it about the city streets and on the subways. My friends and I would take bets on how many times a day someone would mistake me for Susan Reed since she also had long red hair and played "a weird instrument" (the zither). (This was during the time that Burl Ives and Susan Reed were bringing folk music to national attention in night clubs, theaters and on the radio.) Oscar Brand asked me to be a guest on his WNYC Folksong Festival, and the date was set for February 6, 1949. About a week before this time rolled around, Alan Lomax took me to visit in the home of Hudie Leadbetter on East Tenth Street. Leadbelly and his lovely wife, Martha, received me warmly, although he was quite ill, propped up in a chair, and, according to Martha, in much pain. I could never have guessed it; to me he seemed strong and vital, taking keen interest in everything that was said. When Alan told him that I was going to be on the Brand show, he smiled and leaned forward, putting his hand on my arm. "I've sung on that show, and I get that on my radio here! I want you to dedicate a song to me, do you hear? Yes, sing one for me. I'll be listening to see you do!" He threw his head back and the chair shook with his big laugh. I did what he asked on that Sunday show, and the following January sang the same song for him again, *Old Virginny*, my father's version of *East Virginia*, at the Leadbelly Memorial Concert, for he died at midnight on December 7th, the dawning of my birthday.

My dulcimer and I became regulars on the WNYC Folksong Festival, beginning in October of 1949, and for almost a year, dulcimer music poured over New Yorkers every Sunday evening at six o'clock. In these studios I met many other performers, including Susan Reed, Tom Glazer, Hally Wood, Lord Invader, Sonny Terry, Reverend Gary Davis, Richard Dyer-Bennett, Tony Kraber, Tom Scott—almost every new (and old) face passing through the city came to that show.

1950 saw a small boom in dulcimer popularity in New York City. I did my first solo concert for the Country Dance and Song Society, at the little Greenwich Mews Theater on March 29th. (I remember amazing the audience by dribbling water from my fingertips onto the dulcimer pegs to keep them from slipping.) In May, I took part in the Sixth Annual Contemporary Music Festival at Columbia University, this one organized and narrated by Sydney Robertson Cowell. The concert featured seventeen Old Harp Singers from Tennessee, Everett Pitt and Sam Eskin singing New York State folk songs; also *three* dulcimer players—besides myself there was Andrew Rowen Summers from Virginia, and Don Baker, who, according to the New York Herald Tribune review of the event, "played a hammer dulcimer favored in the north woods of Michigan." The reviewer went on to conclude. . ."There was a striking contrast between the soft tones of the southern mountain dulcimers. . .and the brighter, more assertive Michigan dulcimer on which Mr. Baker played *Make Haste to the Wedding, Turkey in the Straw,* and *The Irish Washerwoman*. I am sure this was the biggest dulcimer invasion that New York had ever seen up until that time.

As the year went on, life became even more exciting and interest in the dulcimer continued to build. Mr. Lomax introduced me to the people at Oxford University Press and they gave me the go-ahead to begin work on a book about my family and our music (this was to be *Singing Family of the Cumberlands,* which did not see publication until 1955). On a soft June evening in the Lomax apartment, I met Alan's sister Shirley from Texas, Frank and Ann Warner (first collectors from Frank Proffitt and many other important eastern singers, and Frank could sound almost exactly like the singers from whom he had collected), and Carl Sandburg, singer, folk song collector, poet, and biographer. What music that night! In September, my heart and hand were won by a handsome young New York photographer, George Pickow.

We had met the year before at one of the Henry Street Saturday-night square dances, led by that incomparable Tennessee caller, Ralph Tefferteller. Actually, thinking back on things, the dulcimer was responsible for my marriage, because a girl friend of George's had lured him down to the Settlement square dance by telling him about a Kentucky red-head who played this strange instrument and sang old songs. During intermission that night, I sang a few family songs with the dulcimer, and George, who was a collector of Bessie Smith records, thought I was too unreal for words and wanted nothing to do with me, but asked me to dance anyway; then he asked me to go dancing the following week at Michael Herman's, and so it developed until I took him to meet my family in Kentucky (this was the summer of '49), and while there, he looked at several dulcimers, visited Jethro Amburgy, and decided to build one himself. Using what he had learned from studying Jethro's and Dad's old Thomas dulcimers, he designed and made a most beautiful one, and told me it was for "the girl I marry, whomever she may be." Of course I said "Yes" at once then. We were married on September 29, 1950.

In December of this magic dulcimer year, Haverford College, in Pennsylvania, invited me to do a recital; there I met a young student named Jac Holzman who was delighted with the Ritchie family music and stories. I told him that my friend Edward Tattnall Canby had been doing some recordings of my singing in New York; later, the recording sessions continued in both the Canby and Holzman living rooms. Jac and his partner, Paul Rickholt, had started a little record company with the issuance of an album of avant-garde art songs which had not sold well; so the eventual result of our recording sessions that winter was Elektra Records' first folk music album, a 10-inch lp entitled *Jean Ritchie, Singing Traditional Songs of Her Kentucky Mountain Family.* Thus, in 1950 the dulcimer, Jean Ritchie, Mrs. George Pickow, and Elektra Records were all well launched.

By this time I was going out to colleges and cultural groups in ever-widening circles, and in 1952, while a recipient of a Fulbright scholarship to study folklore in the British Isles, I was invited to represent the USA at the International Folklore Conference, held that year in Biarritz and Pamplona in the Pyrenees. George, in addition to his photographing assignments, helped enthusiastically with folksong collecting, the instruments, tape recorders, and managing the trip. I helped him take pictures, and wrote some stories and captions (I once had to defend him to the British press when he and a custodian left a ladder inside the clock tower and stopped Big Ben).

Everywhere we went, the dulcimer helped ease the way, insuring our welcome in village square, kitchen and banquet hall. Musicians throughout England, Ireland, and Scotland held parties and ceilidhs whenever we came, singing and playing their best music for us. We made the first recordings of many people who later came to be well known in the folklore field, including Frank McPeake and his family of Belfast; Jeannie Robertson and Jimmie MacBeath in Scotland; and Tommy Makem, then a young boy, still at home with his family in Keady, County Armagh in Northern Ireland. In London, a young playwright, Ewan MacColl, recorded for us some of his own new "folkstyle" compositions, as did the lovely actress Isla Cameron, and a sweet-natured gentleman whom we knew only as "Bert" for days before learning his full name, A. L. Lloyd. We spent many happy evenings at the flat of our good friend, folklorist Peter Kennedy who, with

George Pickow.

11

Seamus Ennis, was then doing the great body of collecting for the British Broadcasting Corporation, and who sent us to dozens of beautiful singers throughout the Isles.

Coming home to the United States in 1953, George and I settled down to build a life together. He became a specialist in color photography, I continued concertizing around the country and writing and recording; together we produced several documentary films on folklore. Television was a shining new medium, and I too, my dulcimer on nearly all the early shows which had guest spots; on some I did the entire show, sort of a primitive special. Some of these shows were "Today," with Dave Garroway, "The Fitzgeralds," "Wide, Wide World," "Lamp Unto My Feet," and "Camera Three." Letters came from all over the country; people wanted to know more about "that strange lovely instrument," and where to get one. About 1956, I started going to the Berkeley Festival in California, and the dulcimer had bridged the country.*

By this time so many of our own friends had wanted dulcimers, that we had to do something about it. Up until that time I had been directing people to cousin Jethro Amburgy and to my long-time friend Homer Ledford, both in Kentucky. Now, folks began to demand that we make dulcimers like our own, George's design. We began to build them in our basement in 1959, and brought in Uncle Morris Pickow to help, because neither of us had time to treat dulcimer-making as anything more than a hobby. Uncle Morris was pleased to have this opportunity; he was having trouble doing his regular work because of his arthritis. In a very short time he was doing all the body work, while George helped with artistic decisions and finishing, and I sanded, placed the frets and approved each instrument. Uncle Morris was a careful, enthusiastic craftsman, and wanted so much to give folks full measure, that he began unconsciously to make his instruments slightly larger; imperceptably at first, but over the years Morris Pickow's dulcimers grew noticably different from George Pickow's original design. The demand grew as his dulcimers grew better and more beautiful, and soon he needed more room,

so he took molds and tools over to his own home in the Williamsburg section of Brooklyn, under the bridge. Sometimes we would say to people, very solemnly of course, "Oh, yes, they're very traditional—made in historic Williamsburg." Then, when they looked properly impressed, we'd add ". . . under the bridge in Brooklyn!"

Uncle Morris enjoyed making dulcimers more than anyone I ever knew. He loved to see the wood pieces emerge as instruments, and whenever he brought one in for me to set the frets in place, he would let no one make a sound until I had made all the pencil marks, laid the test pins in place and played a tune. A look of absolute joy and wonder would fill his face, as though he had just heard his new baby's first cry. He got great pleasure from meeting the people who came for his dulcimers, and considered each of them his friend. In 1968, his health began to fail, and at last he had to give up working in the little shop and enter a hospital, where he died of cancer in the fall of 1970. He had made 357 dulcimers, all now valuable collector's items.

Meanwhile, amid all of this activity, George and I started a family. Our sons, Peter and Jonathan, were born in 1954 and 1958, adding their own music to our lives. I kept on, whenever family duties would allow, performing at schools, colleges, helping with the folk festivals, large and small, which were springing up and flowering around the land. In 1959, I took part in the first Newport Folk Festival, in company with The Kingston Trio, Earl Scruggs, Pete Seeger, Jimmy Driftwood, Sonny Terry, Brownie Maghee, Frank Warner, Oscar Brand, Leon Bibb, the New Lost City Ramblers, Odetta and John Jacob Niles.

When the Newport Folk Festival reorganized in 1963 as a non-commercial venture, Pete Seeger and Theodore Bikel invited me to be one of seven to make up the original board of directors. The others we chose were Erik Darling, Bill Clifton, Clarence Cooper and Peter Yarrow.

The Newport Folk Festival was the first large eastern festival to make wide use of the small workshop idea. There were ballad workshops, blues workshops, and of course workshops on all the folk instruments. From the beginning, there

*In 1961 George and I, walking across the campus at the Berkeley Folk Festival, were greeted excitedly by a young couple. The boy, whose name I cannot remember, unwrapped from a shawl an *exact* copy of our (George/Morris Pickow) dulcimer. He was just beginning to make and sell them. The following summer, 1962, I taught at the Idyllwild Arts Foundation camp in California. Walter Camp was also there, and he told me that at McCabes Guitar Shop

in Los Angeles, one of our dulcimers had been taken apart and a copy pattern had been made; the shop had then started making its own. I believe that these were the first dulcimers produced commercially in California, and that most of the many subsequent dulcimer-makers around the state took their patterns, or at least their inspiration, from these, including the builders of the Topanga Canyon model.

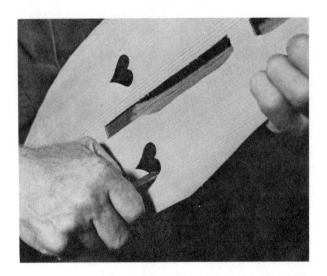

Morris Pickow.

was wide interest in the dulcimer, and it was exciting for me to see my workshop being attended by so many, and some with their own dulcimers slung over their shoulders in a variety of homemade cases, canvas or quilted bags or simply wrapped up in a shawl like a baby. By the 1964 festival, several folks had copies of *The Dulcimer Book* (which was published by Oak Publications in 1963), and had learned to play in my style. More often, dulcimer owners had taken the advice I gave in the book and had made up their own playing styles. No two were ever alike! The special appeal of this instrument seemed to be that there were no rules and very few guidelines or sources of written music. Almost everyone kept his playing style very simple and played traditional music, but once in a while an innovator would come along with a Calypso strum or a fast banjo-picking technique, or would spin off jigs and reels with breathtaking dexterity.

One innovator who caught the fancy of the Newport festival-goers, and people all over the country, was Richard Fariña in 1965, playing and singing at the dulcimer workshop with his new bride, Mimi, whom he had recently met and married in France, shortly after the break-up of his first marriage. I had met him first in the early fifties. My friend Diane Hamilton, founder of the Tradition Recording Company, had invited George and me to a party at her house in New York City. A new folksinger was present, Carolyn Hester, with her husband Dick Fariña who was at that time a magazine writer. He seemed very shy, but got quite excited about our dulcimer, examining it and trying a few strums on it, saying he would like to learn to play one. Later on, while visiting Paul Clayton in Virginia, he listened to and played dulcimers with Paul, A.W. Jeffries and their neighbors, and his own unique style evolved.

Richard Fariña was born on the high seas between Cuba and New York, and he died in a motocycle accident on May 1, 1966, in California.

His use of the dulcimer with the new music of his time—his own songs and those of other contempories, captured the attention of a whole new segment of the population, the thousands of young followers of the folk-pop idols in the Big Festival Era of the 1960's.

Performing at the Greek Theatre, Berkeley Campus, as a participant in the annual student-produced Berkeley Festival, in 1963 or 1964.

Richard Fariña.

It was not only in America that dulcimer fever was spreading. In England, John Pearse, a young man who saw his first dulcimer, ours, at Peter Kennedy's London flat (in 1960 when we were on a second visit), began to build the instrument, play and give instruction. In 1970, his dulcimer book was published in London (see bibliography).

John Pearse's reaction to the music is typical of what had begun to happen in many parts of the world. People write to us now from France, Australia, England, the Scandinavian countries, Wales, Israel, Alaska, Iceland, Germany, Austria, Holland, Yugoslavia, Roumania, Japan, Hawaii, South American and Central American countries, Spain—every day new postmarks and new friends, and what a stamp collection we have! They ask about getting a dulcimer, about learning to make their own, tell us about songs, wonder where they can buy books and records, inform us about other dulcimer makers and players, say hello and invite us to visit; and often, they write just to say they have our book and like it very much.

All of these people around the world, those of us in the present and those in the past, I like to think of as a band of friends; and for the lack of a better name for this little band, I call us the Dulcimer People. Some of these friends I would like to introduce and talk about in this book. A few of them are famous; some are comparatively unknown. Some have departed this life but will be with us as long as a dulcimer rings in a home, a concert hall, or under a tree somewhere. Others are new young people who have fallen early under the spell of this music. And there are thousands of others whom I don't know yet, or know too little to tell about. Some of them make dulcimers but don't play them; some play dulcimers but don't make them; some do both. One wonderful thing seems common to all true Dulcimer People —they don't mind sharing their knowledge of the instrument and its music with others; in fact, they get great pleasure from this sharing. This book is an attempt to gather as many of these friends as is possible; to name them, to categorize them (gently), to talk about their specialties and interests insofar as we know them, and to listen and learn from those who have wanted to talk, in their own words. One will tell us how to make dulcimers and assemble kits; two will describe in detail the various tunings they have discovered, and how to use them; from others we will learn the best and quickest ways to "jam" with other instruments; several will give examples of their own highly interesting and often intricate styles.

The Dulcimer People

Pioneers Past and Present

Dulcimer People nowadays spring up any-where, in city or country, from mansions or from the depths of poverty. I guess poor people like the instrument because it is something they can afford or make themselves, and if they haven't been educated in formal music, the dulcimer doesn't care. Richer people are more likely to have had musical training, but the little three- or four-stringed monochord appeals to many schooled musicians because of the challenges of its limitations—and sometimes, perhaps, because it sings of times and places where life was simpler and better. For, do with it what you will, manipulate its strings in as complicated a way as you know how, and its voice will still sound out as itself, straightforward and honest and lovely.

In older times, the Dulcimer People lived, as near as I can tell, in one region of our country, the Southern Appalachians, mainly in mountainous sections of Kentucky, North Carolina, Virginia, West Virginia, and Tennessee. From there they spread quickly to the surrounding states, Ohio, Indiana, Missouri, Arkansas and Georgia. To keep our dulcimer story as chronological as we can, let us start out with the oldest Dulcimer Person we know, and then meet some of the other pioneers and their families, past and present.

J. Edward Thomas

J. Edward Thomas in 1924, taken at Ball, Ky. in front of his house.

(Note: Mr. Thomas, Will Singleton, and Jethro Amburgy are written about in *The Dulcimer Book*. However, for those who may not have seen this book, I shall quote here from time to time excerpts concerning these three).

J. Edward (Uncle Eddy) Thomas is the earliest dulcimer maker and player that anyone has been able to trace for certain in this country. He was born in Letcher County in 1850 and lived most of his life in the little village of Bath, Kentucky, some twenty-five miles from the Ritchie home in Viper, Perry County. He began making dulcimers in 1871.

James Still, noted Kentucky poet-novelist and a resident of Dead Mare Branch, near Bath, since 1929, gives these additional notes on "Ed'ud" Thomas, which greatly helps us to see the man, his place, and his time: "Bath, which was my post office as well as Thomas's, was discontinued about five years ago. The post office serving us by rural route is now Mallie, some nine miles away, and as we say it, 'way over and gone to Hell on Troublesome.' The Thomas place was on the Big Doubles, under the Bell Coney Knob, which sits astride the Knott and Letcher County lines.

"I know several people who knew Edward Thomas all their lives and last year while making a collection of local 'biographies'—for no purpose in particular except it was in some cases the last moment to do it—I talked to these persons about Thomas and recorded their remembrances. I plan to do more on Thomas, also interview some of his grandchildren when I can get up with them. He was a unique personality. Anticky. Comical. Liked a joke on himself as well as others. Delighted in pulling a rusty. And as for his dulcimers, I have descriptions of how he made them. And he is the only person anybody remembers making them in his day.

"Dad said it used to be a common sight, when he was a little slip of a chap, to see Thomas' (sic) dulcimore cart go up and down the creek roads in the summertime. He had a little kind of frame made and he hung his instruments around that frame. He'd go along, meet someone in the road, say howdy and invite the person to sit on the roadside and enjoy a little tune. Yes, he kept a chair hooked to the cart, and he'd take that down and sit in it and draw the dulcimore crost his knees and he'd make the mountains purely *ring* with that music. Then, he'd stop at houses, too, and show off his dulcimores. If twas near dark he'd stay and take the night with the family and he'd play music on their porch for them till ever so late. Yes, folks allus liked to see Thomas come."

Dad told me that Uncle Eddy liked to get about six dollars for a dulcimer, if he could, but that he'd sometimes swap things for them, if folks had no money. He usually numbered his instruments, too, and signed his name. Mine is not numbered; the handwritten inscription reads: Manufactured by J.E. Thomas, Bath, Kentucky, March 13, 1917.

Allan Eaton, in his book, *Handicrafts of the Southern Mountains* (Russell Sage Foundation, 1937) said this: "He began making dulcimers when he was twenty-one years old, continuing. . . until shortly before his death in 1933. . .he may have made as many as 1,500 all told. There is no record showing exactly what disposition was made of all of these, but probably Mr. Thomas' statement that 'they went to all lands everywhere' is not too vague if we think of all lands as meaning the United States and England. . .His nephew said that at one time 'Uncle Eddy' had made a dulcimer for the Prince of Wales. . .and that 'the King' had written him a nice letter with 'a lot of gold and purple on it,' but one of the children burned the letter by mistake, 'so he couldn't show it to any one any more.'

"Mr. Thomas made his dulcimers out of walnut though sometimes of maple or birch, and a few of California redwood which he said came from 'far over the seas.' His favorite design for the sound-holes. . .was heart shaped. The decoration around the heart is painted in gold on a few of his instruments."

One more bit of information about Uncle Eddy came to me just recently from a surprising source, in a letter from Arkansas dulcimer maker Lynn McSpadden (see p.   ). He wrote, "Our pattern is based on one sent to Arkansas in 1923. The maker was McKinley Craft, in Bath, Kentucky. The dulcimer. . .was sent to Joe Craft (now eighty-two years old), a respected moonshiner in the area. One of Joe Craft's closest 'business associates' was a half brother of Edward Thomas. Small world!"

Small world, indeed, and this helps to confirm my theory that dulcimers got their start (in this country at least), if not solely from Thomas, then almost certainly in the "Appalachian cradle" of Kentucky, West Virginia, Virginia, North Carolina and Tennessee. (I lean toward thinking that Kentucky was earliest, but perhaps that's because I'm a Kentuckian)—in the ruggedly mountainous parts of those five states that point in toward each other, and then spread outward with migrations of mountain people looking for more fertile land, better jobs, and an easier way to live.

Will Singleton

Uncle Will and Aunt Vesta Singleton, Viper, Ky.

"In Viper, where we lived, the dulcimer maker was Uncle Will Singleton, whose old-fashioned white frame house set just over the river from the post office, at the other end of the swinging bridge. Uncle Will had a large kindly face framed by a shock of silky white hair, and a tremendous mustache to match. He was a big slow-moving man, easy of nature, always dressed neatly even at home, with suspenders, the mark of a gentleman.

"Uncle Will's dulcimers were usually oblong or gently curved, generous in size. Uncomplicated and ample, like himself. His shop was in the woodshed out behind the house, and when he finished up an instrument, he brought it into the living room and hung it on the wall until someone came to buy it. Oftentimes there would be seven or eight dulcimers hung about the walls, lying on the fireboard. He loved to take them down and play them, first one and then another, until he had heard all their voices. He played for himself, whether anyone else was there or not, but if you came visiting and asked him to play, you only had to ask him once.

"At our annual Hall Reunion (he was kin to the Halls, and my own mother's maiden name was Hall) he was a familiar figure, dressed in black for the occasion, sitting on the speakers' platform under the trees with his dulcimer on his lap, playing and patting the rough boards with his foot for the entertainment of the company. There would be two or three hundred people assembled, each family with its good-smelling dinner basket, on the wood plank benches around the hillside. Oaks rustled and bees buzzed, babies cried gently, old ladies fanned, the dulcimer droned and remembered."

For all the years of my growing-up and knowing Uncle Will, I never thought to ask him where he learned to make the dulcimers that were so much a part of his life, and it seems no one else did either. It is my guess that he made up his own pattern after seeing those of Ed Thomas, leaving off the double curve so that they'd be easier to shape, and cutting diamond-shaped holes instead of hearts for the same reason (some of his later ones did have hearts). Again, from, *The Dulcimer Book:*

The song that I recall his singing most often was a favorite of his wife, Aunt Vesta: *We're Floating Down the Stream of Time.* His style of playing was like my Dad's (Balis Ritchie) and Ed Thomas's, using the noter and the turkey quill pick. I've tried to set it down for you here in tablature for dulcimer with the good help of our son, Peter. The tuning is major (see My Own Basic Tunings, p. 61), and it's a grand old song. Try it now or after you have read Peter's note on tablature.

A Note about Tablature for the Ritchie Songs

by Peter Pickow

Tablature is a way of writing music for a specific instrument. In the case of the dulcimer, the tablature indicates which strings and frets are employed while conveying the rhythm the same as in conventional musical notation (i.e. quarter notes, eighth notes, etc.).

There are two basic types of tablature used in this section, and for the other songs which I have transcribed, on pages 88-104.

1 *Strumming tablature.* Used when the melody is being played on one string, the others are left unfretted, and all are strummed together with a rhythmical motion using a pick. Indicated by "И" or "H" clef. Quarter, eighth, and sixteenth notes indicate the strumming rhythm; numbers above tell where to fret the first string; arrows above indicate which way to strum: downward arrow (↓) toward you, upward arrow (↑) away from you.

2 *Finger-picking tablature.* Used when strings other than the first are fretted, and plucked individually. Indicated by "T" clef. Three lines symbolize the three strings of the dulcimer, the bottom line being the closest, the melody or first string. Numbers refer to frets. For example, would mean that the first string is to be fretted at the third fret. Rhythm is indicated by assigning quarter and eighth note values to the numbers: "8 " = quarter note, "12 " = eighth note, etc.

Any variations in these formats is explained at the particular place it appears. The melody, written out in conventional notation, for those who read music, is provided for all pieces as an aid to learning the tune.

We're Floating Down The Stream Of Time

Traditional. Arranged by Jean Ritchie

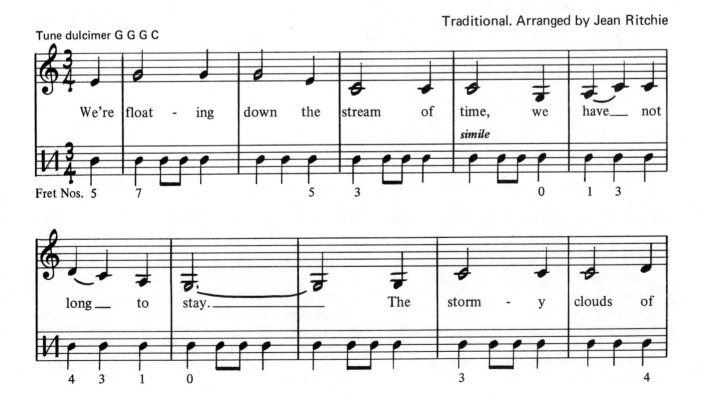

Tune dulcimer G G G C

We're float - ing down the stream of time, we have＿ not
simile

Fret Nos. 5   7   5   3   0   1   3

long＿ to stay.＿   The storm - y clouds of

4   3   1   0   3   4

dark - ness will turn to bright - er day.

— Then let us all take cour - age for we're — not

left — a - lone. — The life - boat soon is

com - ing to gath-er the jew - els home. —

Chorus
Then cheer, my brother, cheer, our trials will
    soon be o'er,
Our loved ones we shall meet, shall meet upon
    the golden shore.
We're pilgrims and we're strangers here, we're
    seeking the city to come.
The lifeboat soon is coming to gather the
    jewels home.

The life boat soon is coming, by eyes of faith
    I see,
As she sweeps through the waters, to rescue
    you and me,

And lands us safely in the port, with friends we
    love so dear,
"Get ready," cries the Captain, "Oh look, she's
    almost here!"

Oh, now's the time to get on board, while she
    is passing by;
But if you stand and wait too long, you may
    forever die.
The fare is paid for one and all, the Captain bids
    you come,
And get on board the lifeboat, she'll carry you
    safely home.

We're Floating Down The Stream Of Time

Tune dulcimer CGG
(for a four string dulcimer fret
the first two strings as one)*

Traditional

*This can be done by cutting notches in the bridge and the nut about 1/8" away from the first string notch, then loosen the second string, place it in these notches, and tune it up again to unison with the second string.

Jethro Amburgy

Jethro Amburgy

Since Jethro Amburgy is the direct descendent —the next in line— in the "Thomas Family" of dulcimer makers, we'll introduce him here, although some builders in other parts of the country are earlier. Jethro was born and raised in Knott County, my father's county of birth, in the town of Hindman, some forty miles away from where we now live, in Viper, and he was a distant kinsman to us Ritchies.

As a young boy attending the Hindman Settlement School he was acquainted with dulcimers, for Mr. Thomas was a frequent visitor to the village and several folks around the Settlement owned and played the instrument. Soon Jethro decided to make one, and Thomas gave him his own pattern and helped him get started on it around 1920 or 1921. The Hindman School taught the native crafts, weaving, basket-making, chair-making and caning, and all kinds of wood-work; so, when he was in his late twenties, probably about 1931, Jethro was hired to teach in the woodworking shop. There he taught the mountain students to make dulcimers over a period of about thirty years. He always made one design, the slender, lovely three-stringed instrument that Ed Thomas had passed on to him.

Jethro's method of playing was rather unique for his time and place. He used the noter, but his right hand, instead of striking the strings with the traditional goose or turkey quill, picked the strings with his fingers the way a banjo-picker does. Once, while visiting in his house as a young girl, I heard him humming as he played. Sometimes a few of the words would escape through the humming, but when he saw that I was listening, he stopped his soft singing. It had sounded so good, I begged him to sing again, but he never would, saying he was "not a singer." I asked different members of his family if he ever sang around the house, but none of them had ever heard him.

This seemed curious to me, and more so when I began to notice that my own father, who learned to play from Thomas, also never sang with the instrument. He had a good voice, and sang in the Old Regular Baptist Church, strong and clear, and he hummed and sang ditties around the work all the time, but when he sat down with his dulcimer, he'd often play all the verses of a long ballad but never utter a word nor hum a line. It was as though the instrument were singing the song and he was listening. I don't know for sure, but I suspect that most folks at that time were so used to song as being an unaccompanied thing, that it hadn't occured to them that singing and instrumental music could go together! (Uncle Will Singleton was the one exception to this "rule" in my memory, and it was probably his example that inspired my youthful experiments with singing to dulcimer accompaniment.)

Jethro Amburgy died in the fall of 1971. People all over the mountains and throughout the country had bought his dulcimers. He made many of them before he started putting numbers inside, but the last numbered one at the time of his death was 1138.

Jethro's directions for making a dulcimer may be of interest. These were contained in a letter to his friend James Still some years ago.

How to Make a Dulcimer

The first step in making a dulcimer is to select the material. The varieties of wood I use in making a dulcimer are several. The most common ones being black walnut, maple, poplar and cherry. I use black walnut, maple and cherry; all make nice dulcimers. In going about making a dulcimer I first select a peice of material that is well dried as it comes from the mill. Seven separate pieces of material go into the finished dulcimer exclusive of the three pegs; the head, tail piece, two sides, top, bottom and the finger board. All pieces are finished according to a design handed down for generations and then assembled and put together with glue. The only tools I use are saw, brace and bit, plane and pocket knife. The pocket knife being the most valuable. The bottom and top are made of material six inches broad, sawed with a hand saw as thin as possible and then finished to about 1/8 in. thick with a plane. After all pieces are gotten to the right thickness, then the pocket knife is used to finish the design, and then glued together.

Benjamin Hicks

Benjamin Hicks and family.

Benjamin Hicks, considered the father of the "North Carolina Dulcimer Family" (my own title), was born in the Blue Ridge section of North Carolina in 1870, and died there in 1945. He did farming and wood carving all his life. According to his son-in-law, Edd Presnell, who learned the trade from him, Benjamin's younger brother Brownlow Hicks actually made the first dulcimer in that area, after seeing one owned and played by a man named Millard Oliver who "passed through about seventy-five or eighty years ago," which makes the date somewhere around 1892. No one knows where Mr. Oliver got his dulcimer (except that he did not make it himself), nor where he came *from*, or went on to after he "passed through." Conceivably, the Oliver dulcimer *could* have been made by Ed Thomas, since Thomas began to make dulcimers about the time Benjamin Hicks was born (the timing would be right; he would have been a young man in his early twenties when Millard

Oliver came to the community), and since Oliver is a fairly common name in Eastern Kentucky. *If Oliver came from the Kentucky or West Virginia direction, then chances are very high that it was a Thomas dulcimer he carried.*

Apparently, Brownlow Hicks did not keep on with instrument making, but Benjamin did, and became *the* dulcimer maker for that area, as Will Singleton was in ours. The craft was passed on to other members of his family, notably to his son Nathan Hicks whose daughter Bessie married Frank Proffitt, and whose sister Nettie married Edd Presnell.

Edd Presnell

Edd Presnell and his wife Nettie (Hicks) Presnell both play dulcimers. Nettie learned to play about 1925, from her father Benjamin Hicks and her sister Sarrah. After she and Edd Presnell were married, Edd decided to see if he could build a dulcimer, and he completed his first one in 1935. The design is his own, patterned after the early ones he had seen in the Hicks family, a small, slender light instrument, curiously like those of Ed Thomas.

Edd insists that he doesn't play very much, only just for fun, and that Nettie is the player of the family. When he does play, he uses noter and pick, and among his favorites are *Short Life of Trouble, Boll Weavil,* and *The Roving Gambler.*

Nettie Presnell plays in the same style, for fun, to demonstrate the instruments to Edd's customers, and professionally at folk programs and festivals. She loves to play hymns, fiddle tunes, and bluegrass, but does not sing. In 1956, she participated in the recordings for the Tradition Recording LP *Instrumental Music of the South Appalachians.* At the Newport Folk Festival dulcimer workshop some years ago, this is how she picked, *Wildwood Flower.**

*See note on tablature, page 19.

With Stephen Cicchetti (guitar builder) in 1973.

With Nettie Presnell, Banner Elk, North Carolina.

Edd Presnell

The Pale Wildwood Flower

Traditional. Arranged by Jean Ritchie

O he told me he loved me, and promised to love,
And to cherish me always, all others above;
Now he's gone with another, my misery to tell,
He has sent me no letter, no word of farewell.

Yes, he told me he loved me, and called me his
flower,
That was blossoming for him, and brighter each
hour;

When I woke from my dream then my idol was
clay,
For his love like a vision had all vanished away.

I will dance, I will sing, and my smile will be gay,
I will charm every heart, at the ball I will sway;
And I'll live till I see him regret this dark hour
When he's gone and neglected his pale wildwood
flower.

The Proffitt Family

Frank Proffitt at Pinewoods Camp, Buzzards Bay, Mass., in 1962.

William Wiley Proffitt made his first dulcimer at the age of twenty-two, about 1905. The following quotation is from a letter written by Frank Proffitt, Jr., remembering the words of his father, Frank, Sr. The description is of William Wiley Proffitt:

"My earliest memories were of awakening on a cold winter morning and hearing my father play a slow mournful tune on his dulcimer. I loved to lie in bed and dream of someday owning my own and being able to play this truly beautiful creation of the hand of man and God. His voice came sweetly through the frosty air, singing in the sweet by-and-by, we shall meet on that beautiful shore. I looked on my father as the greatest man on earth." No mention is made of where William Wiley learned to build the instruments, but I guess we can safely assume that he learned from Brownlow and Benjamin Hicks, who had started making them some twelve or thirteen years before.

Frank Proffitt, Sr., says his son, probably began crafting the instruments in his teens—a close guess would be somewhere near 1930. Throughout most of his younger years, however, he was better known for his singing and his fretless-banjo and guitar playing.

Frank and Anne Warner, collecting folklore in the region, visited the Hickses and the Proffitts in 1938. This was the beginning of a long friendship, and their interest drew Frank Proffitt's attention back (from the absorbing problems of bringing his young family through the depression years) to his music and his instruments. He started making dulcimers again, and improved and developed his own well-known playing technique. After the Kingston Trio popularization of Frank's song, *Tom Dooley*, in 1959, his life changed.* He became Frank Proffitt, famous dulcimer and banjo maker and musician; he made records, and was sought for all the important festivals including Chicago and Newport. Yet he found time to come to small ones, like our folk music week at Pinewoods Camp in Massachusetts, where so many of us came to know him well, cherishing him for his deep sense of tradition, and his gentle wit and wisdom.

Frank Proffitt, Sr., died suddenly in November of 1965, at the age of fifty-two. He is still with us.

His playing method was in some ways unique. Basically, he used a banjo-picker's strum, as did Jethro Amburgy, and although it produced a flowing rhythm that sounded simple, his left-hand action was more complicated than Jethro's. Frank noted with his fingers, and, in addition to the chording which both of them played, his occasional "hammering-on" of a note, or use of little surprising slides created a sound very much his own. It has been widely copied and built upon by such later players as Jeff Davis (of Pinewoods Camp, and the Guitar Workshop on Long Island), Mary Faith Rhodes (now an important part of the dulcimer revival in France), Richard Fariña (a more indirect influence), and, of course, Frank Proffitt, Jr.

---

*They had found it in a collection compiled by Dick and Beth Best, printed without credit or source. The Bests had heard Frank Warner sing it in concert.

Frank Proffitt Jr.

Ballad Workshop

Frank Proffitt, Jr., is continuing the family traditions; he sings and plays the old songs, the newer ones composed by his father and some by himself. He is also carrying on the dulcimer craft which he has inherited.

The dulcimer he builds is from the family pattern, a slender 'hour-glass' shape, with diamond or heart-shaped sound holes. He has been working at dulcimers since he started helping his father when he was about twelve years old, in 1958. I met him about 1963, when we both performed on a program in Gatlinburg, Tennessee; in 1968 he came to the Newport Folk Festival, where his quiet music and manner more than held its own against the rising "rock" elements which were so prevalent that year.

Frank Proffitt, Jr., at the Newport Festival (Ballad Workshop).

Raymond Melton

Raymond Melton, Woodlawn, Va.

Raymond Melton takes us back in our story a few years, and to another state. One of a long chain of Virginia craftsmen, Raymond and his older brother Jacob (now deceased) became involved with the instrument and its music some forty years ago, about 1932. Their mother, Maggie Melton, played the dulcimer with a fiddle bow, and the instrument on which she played has been in the Melton family for about one hundred years. Raymond says, "I do not know from whom she learned to play, but it was from someone back in the Melton family of long ago I think. She died in 1959, aged eighty-eight. Raymond came to the attention of many of us about 1965, when he appeared at the Newport Folk Festival as part of (of all things) a bluegrass band! I remember that at the workshop I was rather surprised to find that he had all three strings of his dulcimer tuned in unison, and asked him if he played only in the Mixolydian mode. He studied awhile and then said, "Well, I reckon it's easier to keep up with the band that way." I, in turn, couldn't quite see what he meant by that, and proceeded to show him how to drop his bass string down a fifth below the two trebles. He said, "Well, what do you know, I *like* that." He went around showing his friends his "new" tuning, but later on in the day I passed the bluegrass band in action and Raymond's dulcimer was back in the

unison tuning. I slipped away behind the food tent and experimented on my own dulcimer, and sure enough, found that this unison tuning allows one to be more flexible—one can pay in both the Mixolydian and major scales without retuning; also, it is easier to change pitch quickly, a time-saver when playing with other instruments. Many new young players are discovering this secret for themselves, among them my friend Holly Tannen, who has written us a fine chapter on just that. (pages 65-71)

George Moore, Saltville, Va., in 1965.

Ben Dinsmore, Saltville, Va., in 1965.

29

Homer Ledford

Above, Homer Ledford, Winchester, Ky.

Right, Homer Ledford and his daughter, Julia.

Probably the best-known living member of the Thomas Family of dulcimer makers is Homer Ledford, of Winchester, Kentucky. Actually, it was in Brasstown, North Carolina, at the John C. Campbell Folk School, that he first saw and heard the instrument; it was our Thomas dulcimer played by my sister, Edna Ritchie, who was on the staff at the school. That very summer (1946), Homer made a dulcimer in a different shape, an experimental model, and Edna bought it. He might then have made another for himself, and quit, but the Brasstown woodcarvers told the buyer at one of their outlets about it, the Southern Highlander Handicraft Shop (in New York City, but no longer in operation): this shop placed an order for two dulcimers (I worked as a salesperson in this shop for a few months in 1949, and used to demonstrate Homer's dulcimers to customers there). Other shops belonging to this same guild also placed orders, as did neighbors and friends. At last I met Homer, at the first Southern Highland Handicraft Fair held in Gatlinburg, Tennessee, July 27-30, 1949. It was held in a big meadow, under circus-sized tents, and I was on the team of mountain people who entertained the crowds three times a day with play-parties, set-running, square-dancing, and singing. During intermission, I had a solo spot to sing and play

the dulcimer (at that time I had one of Jethro Amburgy's). Music for the dancing was furnished by Clarence Farrell on the fiddle, Philip Merrill on concertina and accordian, and Homer Ledford on guitar. Homer also had his own booth where he showed folks how his instruments were made, and the finished ones were made available in the sales tent. He told me then that he thought he would like to make this his life's work, if only he could manage to support himself.

Now, twenty-odd years later, the Ledford family (wife Colista and three children) own their own home and shop in Winchester, where they all work and play at making fine quality instruments —dulcimers, banjos and guitars (they'll make you a fretless banjo too, if you ask for it). If you attend a crafts fair anywhere in his part of the South, you'll probably see Homer Ledford and his family working in their booth.

He has recently added to his instrument repertoire a "sweetheart dulcimer" (his adaptation of the old twin-fretboard "courtin dulcimer"), and the "dulcitar," which is his own invention: a combination dulcimer and guitar. In addition to instrument-building, Homer and his wife do musical programs for colleges, groups and fairs. He demonstrates his many instruments, plays ballads, and is a lively and interesting speaker for all ages. He has two recordings, a small instruction disc and a later album, *The Ledford Family,* on one side of which the Ledfords have added some songs performed by Edna Ritchie Baker and Floyd Baker (see discography).

Homer's early dulcimer designs were influenced by the Thomas and the Amburgy dulcimers, and by those of John J. Niles. He still makes the traditional shapes, but does not feel bound by them, and has several designs of his own. He will also make instruments to order, to suit the customer's own wishes.

One of Uncle Will's dulcimers.

Edsel Martin

Edsel Martin, of Swannannoa, North Carolina, is of a different family (of dulcimer makers) from the one around Beech Mountain. The Martins are from the Black Mountain area, and Edsel learned the craft from his father, who was a violin maker. The young man learned first how to carve, and carving has remained a foremost interest. Today, he makes a variety of unique creations from wood; the are for sale, for giving to friends, and for his own pleasure. He likes to apply this skill to the scrolls of his dulcimers, making each one an individual personality, an animal, a child, a woman, a bird. He is an accomplished performer, has made commercial recordings and has taught many people his playing style. Two of his prize pupils are Richard and Michelle Heller, whose chapter, "Fingerpicking Melody," appears elsewhere in this book.

New People

Howard Mitchell

The Mitchell Family.

Born in Lexington, Virginia, on February 22, 1932, Howard was graduated from Cornell University with a degree in Electrical Engineering —those are the unimportant details, to put it as he himself probably would. Considering his experience, his natural way with music, and the far-reaching effect he has had on dulcimer people in the last decade, we should list Howard Mitchell ("Howie" to his friends, and that's everybody) with the Old Masters. According to actual dates, however, he falls into the (dulcimer-maker) category of "New People." These categories exist only in my own mind, and so are not anything to be taken too seriously; they just help me to write down the little bit of dulcimer history I know in some sort of sequence. Anyway, I guess that, in Howie's case, we ought to dispense with categories altogether, or make a special one and call him "A New Old Master."

Sometime in the summer of 1956 or 1957, our telephone rang in Port Washington and the voice of a young man wondered if George Pickow, the dulcimer maker, was at home. He would be at home in the evening, I said. "Well," said the voice, "My name is Howard Mitchell. I'm a sailor on leave from an aircraft carrier, and I've made a dulcimer; I'd like to show it to Mr. Pickow and maybe see some he has made, and just talk awhile, and. . ." I told him, sure, come on out and eat dinner with us. He said he'd be on the five o'clock train, that we'd know him by his sailor suit and dulcimer.

Howie confessed later that he thought I'd have hung up on him if he had asked for Jean Ritchie—that he'd hit on that way to meet me—although he wasn't disappointed in George either. Some schemer!

The dulcimer he had made was a good one, but we scolded him a little for using plywood. He explained that he was interested in developing inexpensive easy ways of building the instruments so that poor folks, kids, anyone could have the fun with them. Our argument was that if one is going to put in that much time and effort, one should use good materials. We were all right, of course. Howie, following up on his music-for-all theory, went on to develop the "dulciless," now notorious in song and story as the only cardboard box that was ever played on the concert stage. He experimented endlessly. Not knowing about the old Kentucky "courtin' dulcimer" (maybe he had heard of it—I'm not sure, but I think not), he invented it all over again and christened it, "twi-cimer." Then he turned to and produced some of the finest dulcimers ever made, using the best materials with a fine craftsman's care and skill. An engaging musician, he has made recordings for Folk-Legacy Records, and is the ring leader of a group of singing friends called, "The Golden Ring," in which the dulcimer is used extensively. Folk-Legacy has also produced, along with companion records by Howie, his two excellent "how-to-make-and-play" booklets, one for the Appalachian and one for the hammered dulcimer.

We made tapes that first evening together, and

I'm glad we kept them. We claim a first recording of *In Good Old Colony Days,* along with several collector's items of questionable repute from Howie's life on shipboard with the U.S. Navy.

Where did he get the idea to make dulcimers? He spoke fondly of Dr. Asher Treat, Professor of Biology at City College, who was then living in New Jersey. When I inquired about Dr. Treat in preparing this book, Howie wrote to him and sent me his reply.

Dr. Treat writes: "...in 1931 or 1932...on a visit to my home town of Antigo in Northern Wisconsin I visited some boyhood friends who had immigrated there, with many other rural Kentuckians, around 1900. These people, the Jacobses, had no instruments of any kind, but from them and from reading I learned about the mountain dulcimer. The first one I ever saw was the one that caught your eye and ear years later...it was in unlabelled and unplayable condition in the Longlade County Historical Museum in Antigo, deposited there by someone whose name I've forgotten but who knew nothing about it except that it had been left in his house by a man who had come from the South and was on his way to the Dakotas. Since it had no historical significance (for that area), the curator agreed to release it from the collection, and I was able to buy it for fifteen dollars from the original owner...It is made...not of veneer but of rather thick pieces of wood, stained a deep brown.

"During the war (WWII), my friend Bob Helme sent me another as a gift, one he had bought from the maker, Jethro Amburgy. I believe you saw this one also."

Again, it occurs to me that the originator of Dr. Treat's first old dulcimer could have been Ed Thomas or a neighbor (pupil) of his, since many Kentuckians had, for some reason, gone to Wisconsin, the Dakotas, and the West in general around the turn of the century, when Uncle Eddy was in full swimg as an instrument maker. So, I would say that the Mitchell link probably hangs from the Thomas-Amburgy chain.

A friend of Howie's and mine, Charlotte Williams, a young woman from West Virginia, illustrates this chain effect in an even more intricate pattern. Miss Williams built her first dulcimer in 1964, starting with..."a design from a dulcimer made in Sea Cliff, New York, then designed my own, using pictures from Jean Ritchie's book, Howie Mitchell's book, and dulcimers I had seen in West Virginia as a guide. The Sea Cliff dulcimer would be one made by Åke Tugel, who copied his from Jethro Amburgy, who learned from Ed Thomas. All this with no help from mass media!

Charlotte now lives in Sacramento, California, and is not listed in the "Where to Buy" section because she says that she is at present too busy to make dulcimers for sale.

I have strayed somewhat from the Howard Mitchell story, but that is as it should be; for he, and us others, are but channels after all, taking from the great body of folklore those parts which interest us, illuminating them as brightly as we can for awhile in our own absorption and enjoyment of them, then allowing our knowledge to flow on for others to love and cherish and give. It has been my great joy to have been a part of this process, although in a very quiet way, for so many years, and it is true that in giving and sharing the joy has increased. I like to think that, since my involvement with dulcimers goes back to my childhood in the nineteen-twenties, I can be counted among the old-timers, along with Thomas, Hicks, Singleton, Proffitt, Amburgy, Summers, Presnell, Melton and Niles. With us, the dulcimer put down a firm root and had a steady growth in slowly-widening circles. With Ledford, Putnam, Martin, Mitchell and their generation, running as it did into the jet-computer-mass media age, the dulcimer has realized a Population Explosion.

Howard Mitchell now lives in Washington, D.C. with his wife Ann and their two sons. They don't like the large festivals but can usually be found camping and making music with their friends at the annual Fox Hollow Festival in Petersburg, New York, on the Beers Family farm. Howie does not make dulcimers for sale on a large scale, but builds one on occasion for a friend. He gives us a song, with tablature, later on.

Other New People

Each new dulcimer person that I know deserves much more space than we can give here, but the aforementioned dulcimer explosion being what it is, we must make do with brief mentions of a few of these fine folks.

A. W. Jeffreys

A. W. Jeffreys, Jr. in his dulcimer workshop, 1960, Staunton, Va.

The Appalachian Dulcimer Corporation, in Staunton, Virginia, is one of the early commercial shops. A.W. Jeffreys has been in business there since about 1953, and has steadily grown through the years. The shop has turned out nearly two thousand dulcimers in that time.

For the past ten years, dulcimer making has been a family affair. Mr. Jeffreys and his sons make the instruments, Mrs. Jeffreys takes care of the correspondence, their daughter makes noting bars, picks, and carrying bags and does the packing for shipment. The Jeffreys book, *The Appalachian Dulcimer* was published in 1958.

About one of the old-time instrument makers who lived in Hermitage, Virginia, Mr. Jeffreys says, naming no names, that he wooed his sweetheart by making her a dulcimer and they courted each other playing dulcimers. Said his wife, "We got married and the dulcimer playing stopped."

Besides several old-time makers and players, A.W. knew Paul Clayton very well, and Paul's friend Richard Fariña.

Dennis Dorogi

Dennis Dorogi carries on the dulcimer-making tradition in Brockton, New York, and is another "offspring" of Howie Mitchell. Inspired by the form and sound of Howie's dulcimer, he began to build his own in 1959 and now has a flourishing instrument business. Like Howie, he has great inventiveness, and uses a variety of designs and construction techniques which he has developed. He is a skilled woodcarver, and has recently started making hammer dulcimers and psalteries.

Dennis' playing is very pleasant-sounding. He is one of a growing number of accomplished finger-pickers, and uses the double thumbing banjo style which many younger players favor.

Lynn McSpadden

A. L. Greynolds

People throughout the country know about the Dulcimer Shoppe in Mountain View, Arkansas, and it's owner, Lynn McSpadden, who has been making dulcimers there since 1962. In that time he has made about two thousand instruments, and he knows all the players, families and groups in Arkansas, which is no small feat. In older times in that region, some folks called the dulcimer an "Indian walking cane." No one knows why, since it was not an Indian instrument.

McSpadden's first design was based on one from Bath, Kentucky, made by McKinley Craft (neighbor of Ed Thomas) and sent to Joseph Craft who is still living, although now an old man, in Arkansas. The Mountain View area is the home of Jimmy Driftwood's famed folk festival, an area abounding in dulcimer makers (at least two of them claim to have "invented" the instrument) and players. Lynn supplies Arkansans, and folks everywhere. He has produced, with Dorothy French, an instruction manual and two beautiful and useful song collections for the dulcimer.

When we met in 1964 at a Kentucky folk festival, A.L. Greynolds was part-owner of the Wilson and Greynolds Service Station in Loyal, Kentucky, near the town of Harlan, and was making dulcimers in his auto shop. He had first seen one on an arts and crafts train which toured Kentucky in 1963. It was probably a Ledford dulcimer. He was a good player, but only made thirty-three dulcimers before his death in July of 1968 at the age of sixty-two. His father was a well-known folk singer in West Virginia who performed at folk festivals there almost up until his passing in 1971, at the age of ninety-six.

George Kelischek

When George Kelischek came to this country in 1960, his experience with dulcimer-like instruments had been restricted to the *scheitholt* (see page 50) in his native Germany. He was a master violin maker, but had a great interest in all the medieval stringed instruments as well, and soon established his Workshop for Historical Instruments on Knox Street in Atlanta, Georgia. Here he produced the following: violin, viola, cello, bass viol, *viola da gamba, viola d'amore,* babytone, *fidula, quintfidel, rebec,* psalterium, hurdy-gurdy, lute, Spanish guitar, *scheitholt* (descant, alto, tenor), and lyre. In 1962, he visited the John C. Campbell Folk School in Brasstown, North Carolina, during their summer recorder workshop, and heard my sister Edna Ritchie play the dulcimer. Probably realizing that Americans did not understand the *scheitholt* "ensemble" idea, he designed a single instrument of his own which he called, "the teardrop dulcimer," and began to market it in finished and kit form early in 1963, discontinuing the *scheitholt.*

Mr. Kelischek moved from Atlanta and settled with his family in the Brasstown community, where he continues to produce copies of old instruments (his dulcimers include the well-known double-curved shape now, and some of them feature adjustable frets), and is a dealer in fine recorders, clavichords, virginals, harpsichords, Orff-instruments, accessories, instruction and music-history books, and sheet music. Several of his instruments are available in kit form, including the dulcimer.

Sam Rizetta

Sam Rizetta of Arlington, Virginia, has become well known to many of us recently as an excellent maker of hammer dulcimers. However, he does also make, and play extremely well, the plucked dulcimer, and has this to say about his knowledge of them:

"My first close association with a dulcimer player was with Duane Starcher in Kalamazoo, Michigan. "Dulcimer" meant hammer dulcimer in Michigan, and the plucked dulcimer that Mr. Starcher played was quite a novelty at the time (early 60s). . .the first ones I made were out of my imagination, based on pictures in books where I could see that the fretting was diatonic. I wondered what such an instrument would sound like in my hands—I was much too shy to borrow Mr. Starcher's! I had worked in wood since childhood and was building guitars, so I felt confident that a workable instrument would result."

Of his interesting playing style, Sam says, "I use a noter and a piece of spring wire for a strummer on three-string dulcimers. With the four-string dulcimer, I note with fingers and pluck with one, two or three fingers, depending on the songs. I like to sing Michigan lumbering and sailing ballads. These were usually unaccompanied, traditionally, but a dulcimer gives me confidence."

Sam Rizetta has prepared for the Smithsonian Institution two fine pamphlets on the hammer dulcimer, entitled, *Hammer Dulcimer History and Playing,* and *Making a Hammer Dulcimer.* (These are available to the public as Leaflet 72-4 and Leaflet 72-5.)

William W. Jones

Bill Jones and his dulcimer in front of his workshop in Sunset, Boulder, Colorado, home of the Alpine Dulcimer Company.

At the University of Colorado, in 1958, Bill Jones heard a fascinating sound coming from the auditorium. Following the sound, he saw a person playing a lovely-looking instrument, and Bill was sold on the dulcimer.

Of course, it was not quite as simple as that. It is always a curiosity to me (as you may have guessed by now!) just *why* and *how* these folks became interested in the dulcimer, so I always ask. Bill Jones answers: "Many people have asked me that question. I believe it is the result of all my life; from my boyhood in the Adirondaks, thinking that a square-dance caller on Grand Old Opry must rank in importance near the President of the U.S., through a keen interest in folk music, and strangely enough, through appreciation for the Kentucky rifle (I had a gun-collector relative). I helped restore and build these old-time guns, and I think in doing so I gained a sense of grace, form and how things should be fitted and finished. Years later, as an employee at the Ode Banjo Company, I learned some of the technical ities of musical instrument-making. A more distant influence may be the fact that an ancestor of mine was a cabinet maker and boat builder in

Pen Yan, New York, around the time of the Civil War, and I have his chest of tools which I use today, wooden planes and all.

"While in graduate school at the University of Colorado, I saw a dulcimer, and determined to have one, but couldn't afford it then. The opportunity did not come until 1963 when I had the experience at Ode Banjo."

Bill says his first attempts were pretty bad, but he went on to make others, trying different shapes that he had seen, finally settling on his favorite, which he calls, "the long teardrop." His interest has grown into The Alpine Dulcimer Company, located in Boulder, Colorado, from where at present he supplies two basic models, and will make a left-handed dulcimer for a small extra charge. Another unusual touch he gives is to inlay a silver plate, hand-engraved with the owner's name, into the scooped-out hollow at the right-hand end of the fretboard.

Len and Sue MacEachron   Dave Field

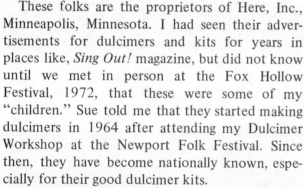

Len and Sue MacEachron on the front porch of their old farm house near the Twin Cities in Minnesota, August 1972.

Dave Field, Pitman, New Jersey.

These folks are the proprietors of Here, Inc., Minneapolis, Minnesota. I had seen their advertisements for dulcimers and kits for years in places like, *Sing Out!* magazine, but did not know until we met in person at the Fox Hollow Festival, 1972, that these were some of my "children." Sue told me that they started making dulcimers in 1964 after attending my Dulcimer Workshop at the Newport Folk Festival. Since then, they have become nationally known, especially for their good dulcimer kits.

The MacEachrons have published a concise, easy-to-understand instruction booklet on playing, with various tunings and sound advice for beginners. From Here, Inc., one can also buy strings, fret wire and tuners, and in addition to dulcimers they make mouth bows, banjos (fretless if you ask for it), and the "bancimer" (dulcimer-fretted banjo!).

Here is one of the first "Mass-media" children—Dave Field, of Pitman, New Jersey, who saw and heard his first dulcimer, "in 1964, on television (played by Jean Ritchie!) I always wanted to play an instrument and this one looked like something I could handle. Then too, I love woodwork and so, in 1965, I started to make my own dulcimer, and have made one hundred and fifty of them, for others. I use my own pattern and design, but I lean heavily on the traditional shapes, the J.E. Thomas in particular."

Dave makes dulcimers as a part-time hobby, and sells one occasionaliy. Like many younger people today, he has been exposed to more than one playing style, and his own is a composite of these, plus what he himself made up. He notes sometimes with fingers, sometimes with a noter, and with his right hand he uses either a pick, or the three-finger banjo style. He likes to play Scottish pipe tunes, American fiddle tunes, and "contemporary songs if they sound right."

Joe Gambill

which he puts into its construction, and to the instrument's role in passing on the traditional music it plays best. He rarely sells a dulcimer, and when he does, the buyer must have a serious interest in folk music, and must promise not to sell the instrument, but to give or will it to a college or museum. Because he feels this way, Joe is not anxious to be listed in the general "Where-to-Buy" section of this book, but, if you'd like to persuade him to make you an instrument, try writing to him in care of the Huntsville Association of Folk Musicians, P.O. Box 1444, Huntsville, Alabama 35807.

As was stated at the beginning of this chapter, dulcimer people come from all walks of life, and Joe Gambill, for someone who likes old music and instruments, has a most modern title, that of Program Analyst for the Research and Development Directorate of Safeguard Systems Command of Huntsville, Alabama. A comparative newcomer to dulcimer building (1968), Joe has been aware of the instrument through his family for over forty years, and actually saw his first dulcimer in 1939 in the Smoky Mountains when, he says, "a man from Kentucky came down and brought one over to a neighbor's house to play. I liked the tone so I bought myself a small one. . ." Then, because he is a large man he tried to have a large dulcimer built, and finally decided to do it himself.

"My first instrument," says Joe, "is similar in size and shape to the Thomas and Ritchie dulcimer. I perfer the sound. . .over the others (Punkin Seed, Tear Drop, and Rectangular Box shapes) although, in the Huntsville area, the old-timers consider only the rectangular box shape a true dulcimer. I haven't yet determined why."

Joe Gambill is sincerely dedicated to the dulcimer, to good old fashioned craftsmanship

Lyn Elder

The Magic Mountain Workshop in Mill Valley, California is owned and run by Lyn Elder, who first saw the instrument being played by Bill Davis at the Charlotte, North Carolina Arts Festival in 1966. That same year, Lyn bought a dulcimer kit from George Kelischek, then living in Atlanta, Georgia, and taught himself to play a little. In 1967, he apprenticed to George Kelischek and started dulcimer making in earnest. In the Kelischek shop, he also learned construction techniques for viols, psalteries and other early instruments. On weekends and vacations, Lyn traveled around rural Tennessee and North Carolina, and his present designs are made up of what he thought was best in the work of the dozens of craftsmen he met, plus what he knew of violin making.

He plays dulcimer professionally as well as for fun, and he favors traditional American, British and Irish music, along with some Medieval and Renaissance music which the dulcimer handles beautifully. Lyn also builds and plays an instrument related to the dulcimer, the hurdy-gurdy, for which he has a fine repertoire of old carols especially suited to outdoor fairs in California at Christmastime. The standard psaltery and the little silvery-sounding bowed psaltery are available from Magic Mountain, too.

New People on Farms and Communes

For many young people today, city excitement can no longer compete with city drawbacks—crowds of folks jammed into crowds of houses set in a sea of concrete bounded by lethal smog.

Well, now that we in the world have become too many, it's easy for us all to see that it would be very nice if each family could have a bit of countryside, fresh air, perhaps a little farm. We are lucky so far in that not everybody *wants* that (some still like the idea of staying in town and minding the store), because there wouldn't be enough to go round any more. But more and more of my young friends *are* choosing to have that acre of land, that country experience. Some

try it for awhile and go back to town; others find their root and tree, and realize a permanent joy in them.

Often, getting the new life going is pretty hard, for farming isn't always enough for survival; so these groups of new land-owners sometimes turn to various handicrafts to supplement their income. Instrument-making has a great appeal, since the making of music is usually an important part of their lives.

Here are two such groups living communally on farms; I have met or learned about them in the course of my travels as a musician.

Seedpod

At the 1972 Mariposa Folk Festival in Canada (Toronto), someone told me about a friend of his, Al McNaught, and gave me Al's address. In reply to my letter, Al McNaught passed on this interesting information about his group on Galiano Island, British Columbia, and their workshops there.

"Seedpod is a group of people living on a small area of land on a largish island off the B.C. coast. At present there are five instrument makers here, specializing in dulcimers and Irish harps. We also find, cut and supply instrument wood of various kinds. This enables us to use the best of the wood we find from a large selection. In dulcimers we use almost strictly red cedar for tops. Backs and sides are of Honduras mahogany, walnut, maple, yellow cedar, rosewood, and ebony. Our instruments are basically hand made. Pieces are rough

cut on a bandsaw or table circular saw. There is no electricity in our shop as yet. Most construction principles are based on Spanish guitar making methods. The dulcimer as a 'local' instrument, apparently came into being here when someone asked Mike Dunn, the guitar maker, to build one for him. He did, wasn't too excited about it, but a demand was created and a few people started building. At present there are nine plus full time, professional dulcimer makers in the Vancouver area. . .the dulcimer production from our shop is already in excess of three hundred. Well over half the ones I make are rosewood back and sides, cedar top. . .usually five strings, two pairs and a single bass. Some fine experimental models have been made using buzzer bridges, loose or suspended fretboards, and sympathetic strings.

Live Wood: P.O. Box 50, Fall Creek, Oregon 97438. From left to right: Sharon Taylor, Richard Stewart, Tom Tonsdelly, Joshua Burt, Deborah Burt, Alison Kerr, Scott Hauser, Sam Jones.

Live Wood

Live Wood is the name given the farm at Fall Creek, near Eugene, Oregon, by eight people living there. Sam Jones and Scott Hauser do most of the dulcimer making, although others help. Live Wood folks also make furniture and do weaving.

Sam Jones has been making dulcimers for about ten years with his two brothers, Calvin and John, in Memphis, Tennessee. While at college (Oberlin), he met Scott Hauser from Slingerlands, New York, who had also been making the instruments about the same length of time,

although they did not work together until the fall of 1971 when Sam joined Live Wood.

About their dulcimers, Sam says, "We have been using walnut, cherry, oak, ash, Tennessee aromatic cedar, and douglas fir. Our dulcimers are mostly a traditional shape with carved scroll, peghead, double curve, and heart soundholes, but we have experimented with different shapes and can make any shape on order. They are usually pretty large (scale length about 30 inches), and we try to make them loud and resonant."

New People Who Teach

Åke Tugel

Not long after Åke Tugel, of Sea Cliff, New York arrived in the United States from his native Sweden in 1956 with his wife Rebecca, he visited a Long Island friend, Henry Salloch and saw there Mr. Salloch's Kentucky (Jethro Amburgy) dulcimer. Within a short time, Åke, who was employed in a shop specializing in cabinet-making and furniture repair, began to make his own elegant copies of the Amburgy dulcimer; and soon they began to be in some demand in his community.

By the mid-1960s, he had his own shop, and interest in his work flourished. As a result of this interest, of his being listed as a dulcimer maker in *The Dulcimer Book*, and of his own personal charisma, young people from all over the country began to seek him out, to ask his advice on dulcimer making, watch him work, and, in general, to pester him pleasantly.

At last, he set aside Saturday mornings for the sole purpose of helping these people make dulcimers. They can buy materials from him, and he lets them use his shop tools and helps them over their crises. One must have an appointment nowadays, as the shop is small and interest is great.

Åke Tugel also sells his own finished dulcimers —the Amburgy design and two others of his own.

Chet Hines

Chet Hines, of Centerville, Ohio, has an ambition a little different than that of other dulcimer makers—he aims to produce a copy of every dulcimer in existence! An ambition that I would say is growing increasingly difficult if not impossible to fulfill. Be that as it may, all his instruments thus far are copies of those he has seen in homes and museums. His favorite, he says, is patterned after W. C. Singleton's No. 79 at Renfro Valley, Kentucky.

The instrument has been an engrossing hobby for Chet since he started building them in earnest in 1946, although he makes his living as a communications engineer at Wright-Patterson Air Force Base. He made his first dulcimer with his grandfather in 1934 or 1935, when he was a little boy living in the Appalachian foothills near Chillicothe, Ohio. As Chet says, "I didn't have a musical instrument so Grandpa Wolfe and I made one—a puny little box and very crude, but it served the purpose."

In 1969, Chet started The Mountain Dulcimore Society, a local group which gathers for occasional weekend camp-ins, and for one large festival each year, usually in September. Chet and his wife Irene opened their shop, The Frontiersman, in the summer of 1972. It features the dulcimer and other wooden and leather handmades by Chet Hines. In addition to performing the old crafts, they also run a dulcimer school which is attended by Chet's customers and dulcimer people in the area.

Dean Kimball

Another Ohioan involved in dulcimer teaching is Dean Kimball of Yellow Springs, though his is a more formal teaching situation. Dean is a professor of engineering at Antioch College, and here is a little of his story:

"Perhaps the most interesting aspect of my dulcimer related activities is that I teach a class in dulcimer making at Antioch College with the able help of my assistant, Rusty Neff. We have conducted this class for four quarters each year for two years past and are now starting our third year (ed.-1972). There are about fifty applicants for the course each quarter. We do not have facilities to handle that many so we put all the names in a hat and draw out 12. Each student makes his own dulcimer starting with raw materials. We do not use kits. It has been one of the most rewarding things I have ever done since the students enjoy and appreciate it so much.

". . .I believe the first dulcimer I ever heard was played when some Berea College students came to Antioch to give an evening of entertainment (JR: the students from Berea were my neices, Joy and Judy Ritchie, daughters of my brother Raymond, who also makes dulcimers). I bought your book and John Putman's. . .in the bookstore at Berea College. I made my first dulcimer starting in September of 1969 and completed it in time to give it to my wife as a Christmas present. I drew my own patterns and design after looking at the pictures in your book. I have since made other shapes."

Dean Kimball does make dulcimers for sale, and also violins and guitars. Being a busy person with varied interests, he does not produce a large volume of instruments (he has made only seven dulcimers in three years), and one would be safe to assume that his dulcimers are more handmade than most, that he is a careful workman and a builder of quality instruments.

Dulcimer People in Other Lands

Often we have wondered whether the dulcimer's ancestors are still in use in their countries of origin; is the *épinette des Vosges* still played in France? The *scheitholt* in use in Germany? The *hummel* in Holland? The *langeleik* in Norway? (See page 50.) Our efforts to find out about these instruments have met with varying success.

My friend Cobi Schreijer, whom I met at the Cambridge Festival in England in 1970, and who runs a folk club in Haarlem (Anslignstraat 29) and knows all about the folklore of Holland, told me that she has seen *hummels* only in museums in her country.

Mr. Vançon, the last *épinette* maker of the Val d'Ajol.

The *Epinette* des Vosges— A Renaissance

In 1952, my husband and I searched for the *épinette* through the French countryside and the antique shops of Paris. No luck in the countryside, but we did find two lovely old *épinettes* in the antique shops. One of the dealers suggested that we might hear recordings of *épinette* music in the Musée de l'Homme. There, to our great excitement, we found listed a recording of *épinette* music performed by an old country woman, the "last remaining *épinette* player." The museum lady proudly *showed* us the record, but would not let us play it because it was made on an early soft disc and to play it would wear it out! We can only hope that by now it has been transferred to tape.

Epinette Makers

Mary Faith Rhodes, an American friend now living and singing with her dulcimer in France, tells us that there is a small revival of interest in *épinette* music, and that copies of the old instruments are being made again here and there. In England in 1960, there were rumors of a touring *épinette* orchestra, but we could never find it. We heard no more until the late fall of 1972, when a young correspondent from Sceaux, Joëlle Andreoli, wrote to me. "Do you know that some people still play the *épinette* in France? I myself have two, but don't play very well. Some of my friends made a film about the *épinette*." She promised details, but time passed and I had already given in the rough manuscript of this book to the publisher when another letter arrived from Joëlle with much information, news of players, and *épinette* tablature; and, as our interest became more and more stirred, two weeks later came another letter from one of the makers of the *épinette* film, Jean François Dutertre, with more details and photographs of players. Both express themselves very well, so with their permission I quote from their letters.

Jöelle wrote: "Unfortunately Jean François Dutertre and Claude Lefèbure are gone on tour for three weeks, but anyway I'll do my best to repeat the information they gave me. There are two types of *épinette* des Vosges: 1) the *épinette* of Gerardmer, and 2) the *épinette* of the Val D'Ajol. These countries are in the Vosges Mountains, of course. The *épinettes* of Gerardmer are made by the Minstrels of Gerardmer, a group of folk musicians. They make them for sale and have all the rights reserved for their model, which is derived from the one traditionally used in this part of the Vosges; they are larger and longer than the others, being seventy to eighty centimeters long with eight strings.

A recent *épinette* from Gerardmer, and one from Val d'Ajol.

"The Val d'Ajol is about seven miles southwest from Gerardmer. The *épinette* here is small, forty to fifty centimeters long (looks like Flemish *épinettes*), and are often much better than the others and more traditional, with five strings. The most famous and best are the ones of Mr. Amé

Lambert, who is dead now. He made about one hundred and fifty *épinettes* a year, helped by his family. They're rare and precious, very beautiful work. He made them all in fruit tree. (JR: I think she means fruitwood.)

"Mr. Jules Vançon is making them now from Mr. Lambert's model. This is the kinds of wood Mr. Vançon uses:

Table in fruit tree (apple or plum)
Ribs in fruit tree
Back in pine tree
Scroll and tail piece in nut tree.

"The frets are placed on a diatonic scale just like the Appalachian dulcimer, but there is no fingerboard; the frets are made of a simple iron thread and planted directly in the table in little holes. (JR: One may also think of it the other way around—that there is no *body*, only a fretboard which was then placed on a table top so as to provide a sound box for amplification. The double-curved body, or sound box, was a later invention.) Violin, hurdy-gurdy, or mandolin pegs may be used.

"Mr. Vançon's *épinettes* are:
64 centimeters long
3.2 centimeters thick
8.5 centimeters wide at the tail
6 centimeters at the beginning of the scroll
15 centimeters is the length of the scroll

"In France, the thin strings on *épinettes* and dulcimers are called *chanterelles*, the bass strings are called *bourdons*. On a five-stringed *épinette* there are two chanterelles and three bourdons. D banjo strings are commonly used for the *chanterelles*, and D, G, and B guitar strings are used for the *bourdons*."

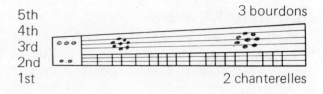

5th
4th
3rd
2nd
1st

3 bourdons

2 chanterelles

46

A player from Val d'Ajol.

Some *Epinette* Tunings

The Major Mode—Three traditional tunings most often used for the five-string *épinette* are:

A. *Chanterelles*   —   G   G
    Bourdons   —   G   E   C

Jöelle does not say which octaves these notes fall in, but I have tuned my own *épinette* to G above middle C for the *chanterelles*, string three (or first bourdon) to the octave G below the *chanterelles*, string four to E above middle C, and string five to middle C. The strings did not break and the sound is pleasant and delightful.

For the eight-string *épinette* the tuning is:

Chanterelles	—	sol	sol	sol	
		G	G	G	
Bourdons	—	do	sol	mi	do
		C	G	E	C

Jöelle does say that your choice of tuning should depend on how high you want to sing. You can also tune to re re re sol; this sounds good with a fiddle.   D D D G

B. A second major tuning is sol sol/sol, sol re
                            A   A   A   A   D

C. A third major tuning is tune all of the strings to the same note in different octaves. This is known as bagpipe tuning.

The Minor Mode

A. fa fa/ sol sol do
    F F G G C (do: middle C, F and G: above middle C. This is actually the tuning for the Dorian mode, with the scale beginning on the sixth fret.)

B. fa fa/ sol sol re
    F F G G D (F, G, D above middle C; a regular Aoelian tuning, the scale begins on the first fret.)

A player from Val d'Ajol with Jean Francois's *épinette*, and a smaller one in front.

Jean François Dutertre ended *his* letter with a tantalizing note, "more to follow;" our deadline prevents the inclusion here of any forthcoming material, but his welcome letter comfirms Jöelle Andreole's and Mary Rhodes' assertions that the *épinette* in France, like the dulcimer in the United States, is indeed having a rebirth. Here is Jean François' account:

"There exist two different regions in the Vosges, in the east of France, each giving the *épinette* a different form and way of playing. In the region of Val d'Ajol, a small valley in the foothills, we find a small model with five strings, from forty to fifty centimeters long. There are about twenty old people who still play, along with the young people who are now beginning to take an interest.

"They use a piece of wood in the left hand and a guitar or mandolin flatpick in the right. The *épinette* is tuned: G G E G C. The drone strings are played rhythmically for the strong beats, attacking from the melody strings. The fretboard is the same as that of the dulcimer. There is still a man who makes the instrument, but mostly for the tourists.

"Farther north, in the region of Gerardmer, we find a larger model from sixty to seventy-five centimeters long. The drone strings are farther away from the melodic strings. At the end of the war there was only one player left, but she has transmitted the tradition to her children. I recorded and took some film of her recently. She also plays with the baton (wooden piece, or noter—see photographs) and a flatpick, or her thumb. However, she attacks the strings from the drones, which are regularly hit on the strong beats. The *épinette* of Gerardmer generally has three melodic strings and from two to four drone strings. The fretboard is either identical to that of the dulcimer, or entirely different. The oldest give an E♭ open; then, going up they sound E, F♯, G, A, B, C, D, E, F, G, A, B, C, D, E, F♯, G. We have found a few instruments with two fretboards on the same body; one we have just described above and the second is composed of all the half-tones missing. The frets run E♭, G, C, E, G.

"At the moment, the instrument is enjoying a certain renaissance among young people, as an extension of folk music. More people are starting to make instruments, especially the *épinette* and the dulcimer. I am preparing a small book on the traditions of the *épinette*. . .which I hope to send to you soon."

Folk Clubs Where *Epinette* Makers May Be Heard

As of this writing, there are three folk clubs in Paris, where one may hear the *épinette des Vosges* and the Appalachian dulcimer played, sometimes now side by side! Here are their names and addresses:

"Le Bourdon" 6, Rue de la Banque, Paris
French, English and Irish folk music. Jean François performs here.

"La Vielle Herbe," 15, Rue Censier, Paris
All kinds of folk music—French American, British, etc.

"T.M.S." (Traditional Mountain Sound), 7 Rue de l'Abbaye, Paris
Mostly American folk, especially old-time country music. Claude Lefebure plays here

It is now again possible to buy an *épinette des Vosges*! See the list of *épinette* makers in the "Where to Buy" section.

Joëlle sent us a traditional folk song from France, for which Jean François has written *épinette* tablature, and she suggests that it may be used equally well on the dulcimer. *La Vieille Fille*, says Joëlle, "is the story of an old maid who had too many lovers when she was young and 'threw them over.' Now she is old and goes to a convent."

La Vieille Fille

Traditional

A quinze ans, j'é - tais gen - till - e, je dé - lais - sais les a - mants,

Je fai - sais la dif - fi - ci - le, à pré - sent je m'en re - pens.

Quat-orze a - mants par se - mai - ne, sont ve - nus _____ m'y sa - lu - er

Un bou-quet de mar - jo - lai - ne, sont ve - nus m'y pré - sen - ter.

Je les renvoyais au poste, c'était mon
    contentement;
Oh! Grand Dieu, que j'étais donc sotte, je m'en
    rends compte à présent.
Quand je vois toutes ces filles, qu'étaient filles
    de mon temps,
Elles ont des maris tranquilles, à leur femme
    bien complaisants.

Voilà mon front qui se ride, et mes dents
    toutes ébréchées,
Mes beaux cheveux qui se grisent, cela m'y
    fait enrager.
J'ai beau porté la dentelle et souvent changé
    d'habits
Les amants ils m'y délaissent, m'y voilà fille
    pour la vie.

Adieu les plaisirs du monde, je m'en vais
    dans un couvent (bis)
M'enfermer avec les nonnes dans un lieu
    d'entroitement (bis).

The Norwegian *Langeleik* —A Mention

The Norwegian *langeleik* seems to be having a similar revival, but we have almost no information about it as yet. Sonia Savig, a lovely Norwegian singer and *langeleik* player in New York City, says that one can now get a *langeleik* made to order, but does not have an address at hand. If you're in Norway sometime, you might inquire at the tourist offices. You may find *langeleik* players, builders, and maybe even a folk festival!

News of the German *Scheitholt*

Hans Bender, California

Hans Bender with the family of *scheitholts*.

Recently, I heard some news about the *scheitholt*. In 1966, Hans Bender, director of the Monrovia Recorder Consort, and owner of the Violin and Recorder Studio of Monrovia, California, wrote to me that he had seen my book (*The Dulcimer Book*), saying, "Now, I think you will be interested to read that we had a group of seven players in Germany and (the instruments were) tuned like a harpsichord." He enclosed a clipping from a local California newspaper showing Mr. Bender with four rectangular instruments of varying sizes. He is shown playing one of them, chording with the left hand and strumming or plucking the strings with the right hand. The caption reads, "A family of instruments called the *scheitholt* is displayed and demonstrated by Hans Bender. The instrument, popular in Germany, is a forerunner of the zither and the various voices are bass, alto, tenor and soprano. When played together they are tuned like a harpsichord."

Before coming to this country, Hans Bender toured Europe as first violinist with the Heidelberg Bach Quartette. The other members of his family are also serious classical musicians. This light shed upon the use of the instrument (that is, that it takes four members or voices to make one complete *scheitholt*) presents a completely different view of the use of our dulcimer, and one to which (to my knowledge) it has never been put in its Appalachian home.

Waldemar Woehl, Germany

Scheitholt: Woehl and Sohne, West Germany

Mr. Bender sent me the address in Germany of the maker of his *scheitholt* instruments, and I wrote to Mr. Waldemar Woehl und Söhne, in Waldböckelheim, West Germany. Mr. Woehl sent us his comments on the *scheitholt*: "While one considers the *glockenspeil* a toy, the *scheitholts* are by today's musical standards, real instruments. The *scheitholt* was mentioned by Michael Praetorius in his 1619 edition of *Organographia*. He calls it a "beggar" instrument, used for the most part by tramps.* Nevertheless, in the following century, the respected zither developed from it."

One cannot be sure, then, without further research, whether the "orchestral" or "four-voiced family" idea was not originated by the Woehl family themselves. Mr. Woehl continues:

"We build the *scheitholts* as an instrumental family: soprano, alto, tenor and bass. Each instrument has four or five metal strings. Basic tuning for the *scheitholt* is D-A-D-G. The ensemble voice produces a very agreeable sound which no other instrument can provide. The instruments are placed on a table, which acts as a resonator. For the plucking of the strings, many people prefer a plectrum. The larger types can be played very nicely with the fingertips, like the harp or the lute, or with the fingernails.

"The *scheitholt* is basically meant for one-voice, one-melody playing, but with more practice one can also play with two or more instruments.** A duet is best performed with the soprano and tenor instruments. For a trio, I recommend two sopranos and one tenor, and the bass is used for the completion of the quartet. Suitable arrangements and orchestrations are available in my publications. A group can play early classical music as well as songs, dances, and accompaniments for singing. Here, we play trios from Haydn and Mozart, five- or six-voiced Divertimenti, Schubert-leider, etc.

"While the *scheitholt* is considerably easier and faster to learn than other wind or string instruments, much experimentation is necessary and it takes awhile until one is a good player. One should therefore not be discouraged after the first few practice sessions, which should be attempted without any help.

"Incidentally, it has been proven that the *scheitholt* does not disturb other occupants of the house. In hospitals, rooming-houses, etc., there has never been a complaint about the *scheitholt*! Also, not unimportant is the very low price, and the ease with which it can be packed and transported—an entire quartet can be lifted effortlessly with one hand! A small instruction manual for each instrument is enclosed, and an extensive *scheitholt* school is in preparation."

With such an irresistable sales pitch, how can I refuse? I'm ordering my tenor *scheitholt* today!

---

*At the Berkeley Festival in 1965, Sam Hinton and I were posing for newspaper photographs on the campus with our instruments. A Korean man passed, and, running back, took out his own camera excitedly. "May I please take your photo?" Then, after he had done so, explained, "I want to show the folks back home—they'd never believe if I told them that *this sort* of musician was being written up in the newspaper. At home, these instruments are played by those who stroll the streets and beg!"

**For our own experiments along this line of ensemble playing, see p. 88.

The Appalachian Dulcimer Puts Down Roots in Israel!

Nuriel Cohen, Jerusalem

The crystaline sound of the Appalachian Mountain dulcimer resounds in the thick stone-walled basement workshop of the "Fiddle-Maker" Nuriel Cohen.

The land of Israel has no history of a native dulcimer-like instrument; it was therefore with some surprise that we heard of a dulcimer maker in Old Jerusalem. One day, out of the blue, came a parcel containing a letter and photographs; on the back of one of the photographs was hand-written this information: "In the thick stone-walled basement workshop of Nuriel Cohen, in Meah-Shearim, the Appalachian dulcimer has had its birth at the hands of this Israeli craftsman."

It was November of 1971 that I received the first letter from Mr. Cohen's friend and now mine, Michael Peyser, a French artist who has chosen to live as a Hassid in the old city of Jerusalem, devoting half his time to painting and half to the study of the Torah. When he was younger Mr. Peyser was interested in the collection of folklore, and has gathered some thousand songs from seven countries. He still loves to sing and make music on the lute, the recorder, and now on the dulcimer. Here is Michael Peyser's story:

"Recently I met a boy from New York who was, before coming to Israel, in California. He spent some time with Kentucky boys, and it was they who sold him his Appalachian dulcimer. I think he had one made by Jethro Amburgy. He possessed also your charming book about the dulcimer, and it was we who gave to our common friend "the fiddlemaker," and originator of the famous Jerusalem guitars, the idea to start making dulcimers also. The suggestions you put forth in your book were most useful to him. He is a born craftsman with golden fingers and I. . .consider myself fortunate to possess the fifth dulcimer that exists in the whole country of Israel.

"His first model was of walnut wood, but the better and improved ones he makes from mahogany. His instruments are shaped rather oblong, but the sound that comes out is very mellow, almost a human voice. You know, he says that he blesses you every morning. He first made dulcimers for his three sons, then one for himself.

"I understood in about one-fourth hour the principle on which the dulcimers work—now what I want is practice. I improvise accompaniments to various songs and even classical pieces; I play certain lieders of Schumann and Schubert, *The Three Gypsies* by Nicolaus Lenau (a German romantic), *The Vegetable Vendor* (a Russian dance), a suite of Mozart, and some German and French folk songs from the Seventeenth and Eighteenth Centuries, all fitting into the Ionian mode. In the Dorian mode I found many old French folk songs such as *La Belle a la Fontaine*, *C'etait la Fille du Labouroux* and *La Belle est au Jardin d'Amour* which date back to the Fifteenth Century.

"A Hebrew name had to be found for the *Appalachian Dulcimer*, to bring it closer to the hearts of the music-lovers of this land. This name is *Naeemah*, which means 'the agreeable, the sweet-sounding.' Nuriel Cohen is confident that with God's help, many 'wandering Jews' and other folksingers from the Holy Land and abroad will learn to love the *Naeemah;* he says that through it the Psalms of King David are awakened to new life."

And *we* say "Welcome to the *Naeemah*—long and lovely may it ring!"

Dulcimer Players Of Note And Some Of Their Playing Styles—

(Honor to the Unknown Keepers)

We owe a great debt, perhaps the greatest, to those rural musicians who never became nationally or regionally known—whose reputations never extended even over the near ridges. These people never sought fame; they found joy in the dulcimer itself. They kept it on the mantlepiece, a treasure to be played as a reward for the days work done; they would leave it there when they moved on down the stream of time, for others to discover. These are the ones who kept the instrument alive singing quietly in a hundred hollers, through a thousand twilights. We can honor them here, but we cannot call them by name, and so we must be content to list those who have come to the attention of a wider audience. They're all fine folks—being known hasn't hurt them any!

Used to be, we could count on the fingers of both hands all the dulcimer players we knew in this country. Not so any more! For now there are dozens, scores, hundreds. We would like to have photographs, life histories, comments and favorite songs from them all, but that's not possible. In this space we'll talk about some of them who play but don't make dulcimers, and have a few of them talk about or demonstrate (as well as can be done on paper) their playing styles.

One of the Unknown Keepers

Some of the Older-Timers

We have already made special mention of Andrew Rowen Summers, John Jacob Niles, the Proffitts, Jethro Amburgy, the Hickses, the Presnells, and all the other early builders we know; and Howie Mitchell and other new players such as Mary Rhodes, the Bender Family in California, and Richard Farina. Here are some others whose playing has had a considerable influence:

Balis Ritchie

This is my Dad, who always said, "Well, I don't know if I can play to do any good" when asked to play, but would then go on to play better than anyone I know. He used a bamboo noter and a feather-quill pick, and performed play-party pieces or any tunes having steady rhythm. We had one of Uncle Will Singleton's dulcimers, and the one by Thomas that Edna had won at Pine Mountain; he taught me to play on these.

Balis Ritchie was born in Knott County in February of 1869, was married in 1895 and died in 1958. The family lived in Knott County for seventeen years after he and Mom were married, before moving to Perry County. He was well acquainted with Eddy Thomas, the roving dulcimer man, and probably learned to play from him.

Here is one of Dad Ritchie's favorite dulcimer songs, *The Uncloudy Day.*

The Uncloudy Day

Traditional. Arranged by Jean Ritchie

O they tell me that He smiles on His children there,
And His smile drives their sorrows all away,
And they tell me that no tears ever fall again,
In that lovely land of uncloudy day.

Note: Dad Ritchie used to sing and hum this song to himself as he paced up and down our long porch in stormy weather, worrying about his corn corp. Here are the verses I remember.

Dr. and Mrs. I. G. Greer

I.G. Greer made his career as a business man in Chapel Hill, North Carolina, but was a collector and singer of folk songs all his life. From his birth in Zionville in 1881 he heard the old songs, and later made a collection of over two hundred of them, from his mother singing at her work, and from neighbors, friends and students through the years.

Mrs. Greer learned to play the dulcimer from her mother, and the instrument she had was made in Watauga County over one hundred years ago. She uses noter and quills.

They performed together since their marriage in 1916, he as a singer and she as the accompanist. In 1929 they recorded for the Paramount Company, New York, and for the Library of Congress, Archives of American Folk Song in the 1940's.

Dr. Patrick W. Gainer

Born in Parkersburg, West Virginia, in 1904, Dr. Gainer has been well-acquainted with folk music all his life. He received his doctorate from St. Louis University in 1933, but never really left home; he has been associated with West Virginia University since the early 1920s.

He had an early interest in the old instrument in use around his home town, and after some inquiry into its history he concluded that it was brought over from England, and was in fact a *rebec*. He says, "The ancient *rebec* is sometimes mistakenly called a dulcimer. It originated in the Orient and was probably brought to England during the Crusades, thence to America with our early ancestors. It has three strings, though only one string plays the melody, the other two serving as drones." That is a scholarly guess, and perhaps as good as any, although I personally believe that the greater body of proof, lore and logic places the instrument in the *scheitholt* family, and its entry into the Southern Appalachians by way of the Pennsylvania Dutch settlers; that the Pennsylvania *zitter* was later named *dulcimer** by some mountaineer with a knowledge of Latin, or, more likely, by someone who had run across the mention of the instrument in the Bible.

Dr. Gainer began his subsidiary career as a lecturer-recitalist in 1928, using the dulcimer, or rebec, occasionally for accompaniment, or to pick a fast fiddle tune. He continues to be active in the folk field as originator of the still-ongoing West Virginia Folk Festival at Glenville, in 1950. His classes in balladry at the University have meant much to many people.

Charles Faulkner Bryan

This noted Tennessean was a fine teacher, scholar, folklore collector, and composer. Born in 1911 near McMinnville, in Warren County, Tennessee, he grew up with traditional singers all around him—his great-grandmother, aunts, uncles and neighbors. He was graduated from the Nashville Conservatory of Music with a bachelor's degree in music in 1934. Because of a keen interest in composing, he went on to study with George Pullen Jackson at George Peabody College for Teachers, and later with Paul Hindemith at Yale University. His compositions include *The Bell Witch, White Spiritual Symphony, Strangers in This World* (a folk musical), and *Singin' Billy* (a folk opera).

He began collecting folk music seriously when he was a young man of about twenty-four, and became particularly interested in the dulcimer. It was a lifelong interest, and he was, in fact, in the midst of concentrated research on the history and origins of the instrument at the time of his death in 1955; his work is uncompleted. However, a series of articles has been published in the Tennessee Folklore Society Bulletin (see bibliography), for which all of us dulcimer people are in his debt.

---

*I have recently learned of a dulcimer-like instrument in Wisconsin (Barron County), played by the Scandinavians who settled the upper Midwest in early days of white colonization. This instrument is called a *salmodikon*, although a few old-timers refer to it as a *notstock*.

Anne Grimes

Born in Columbus, Ohio, in May of 1912, Anne Grimes has sung folk songs since childhood (professionally since 1944), and plays the psaltery, dulcimer, zither, autoharp, banjo and guitar. She has a very large collection of old dulcimers from her region and is considered one of the outstanding experts on the instrument in the United States.

Her album for Folkways, called *Ohio State Ballads,* was issued in 1957, and Mrs. Grimes writes in her album notes: "Most of 'my' singers sing unaccompanied, though there have been a few guitars, banjos and zither-types. The most exciting instrumental discovery has been the traditional use of the strummed or plucked homemade dulcimers. They are also widely known as *dulcerines* in Ohio, to differentiate them from the hammered dulcimers which are also played. And they have even been called *scantlin's* from the lumber they are made of."

Edna Ritchie Baker

Edna Ritchie won her first dulcimer (a Thomas) for knowing the most ballads in the Pine Mountain Settlement School where she was a young student in 1929. She was the ninth child in our family of fourteen, and from the time she could lisp a song, everyone noticed her beautiful, sweet voice. Old folks would say, "I *love* to hear that child sing; now, she can *sing!*" Teachers and visitors from "the beyond" would say, "Your daughter is very musical, Mr. Ritchie; you ought to have her voice trained." So, when Edna followed her older sisters to Berea College, she became the first person in Viper, Kentucky (maybe the first in all of Perry County) to graduate with four years of classical music training—piano, voice, history, theory and composition. When I was a little girl, it was always Edna who was called upon to lead any musical events in the community—school, church programs—and she gave piano lessons to the children between her hours as an elementary school teacher in our little school.

The dulcimer she won long ago was given to Dad, for he liked it so; Edna was more interested in playing our old organ, the piano, and the guitar which was then coming into vogue in the mountains. In 1946, while teaching recorder at the Campbell Folk School in North Carolina, she bought Homer Ledford's first dulcimer, and started using it in public performances of folk music around Kentucky in 1950. Since then she has given hundreds of these performances in many states, and is a cherished teacher and keeper of her mountain traditions.

In 1965, Edna married Floyd Baker, a retired L&N Railroad operator and one of our real mountain-country gentlemen. Soon, to everyone's surprise, Floyd was recalling old songs from his own family, and he began to sing and play the dulcimer with Edna. Homer Ledford presented them with one of his Sweetheart dulcimers, and now they sing and play ballads and courtin'-song duets. You may meet and enjoy the Bakers if you can attend the Berea Christmas School (between Christmas and New Years), where Edna teaches dulcimer and singing games each year, or the summer short-courses at the Campbell Folk School, Brasstown, North Carolina.

Virgil L. Sturgill

Virgil Sturgill of Asheville, North Carolina, with a century-old, 4-string "dulcymore" from Swannanoa, North Carolina.

As a boy, Virgil heard hundreds of traditional songs from members of his family in Carter County, Kentucky, where he was born in 1897; he has been singing for most of his life, although his professional field is education. Virgil learned to play the dulcimer in 1946 from Artus Moser in North Carolina, and he uses it to accompany some of the traditional songs he performs for audiences around the country. (As all good folk singers do, he prefers to sing many of the old ballads without accompaniment.) He uses a noter and feather pick for playing, and his dulcimer was made in Swannannoa, North Carolina, over a hundred years ago. Both he and Artus Moser have recordings of their singing on an album issued some years ago on the Riverside label, entitled *Southern Mountain Folksongs and Ballads.*

John Putnam

John Putnam is a familiar name to dulcimer people. He wrote one of the earliest instruction books, *The Plucked Dulcimer of the Southern Mountains.* It first appeared in 1961, published by the Council of the Southern Mountains, and is now coming out in revised form.

John's interest goes farther back, to the early 1950's when he heard the dulcimer played for the first time. He says, "I was captivated by how easy it was to play this beautiful instrument which I frequently had seen as a decoration in homes." Nettie Presnell influenced him most, and he often plays in her style, using pick and noter; but he also plays with other variations—left-hand chording and right-hand fingerpicking. He sings, too, and prefers traditional children's songs and other southern mountain music. He and his family live in Lanham, Maryland.

Paul Clayton

Paul Clayton playing the dulcimer in front of his farmhouse in the Shenandoah Valley, 1959.

Born in 1933 in New Bedford, Massachusetts, Paul became interested in folk music early in life through the sea shanties of his grandfather. He studied at the University of Virginia with Arthur Kyle Davis and collected songs in the southern Appalachians. He started playing dulcimer in the early 1950's and recorded albums for Stinson, Elektra, Riverside, Tradition and Folkways, using dulcimer accompaniments on some of them. He was a widely known and respected performer, composer and collector. He died on March 30, 1967.

George and Gerry Armstrong

George and Gerry have been mainstays in the Chicago folklore picture for the past twenty years, have given hospitality to every other singer passing through town, and have helped with the Old Town School of Folk Music since its beginnings. Early pupils of Howie Mitchell, they play single and double-dulcimers, usually in the chording-fingerpicking style. They are charter members of the singing group *The Golden Ring*, and have recorded albums with that group and a solo album for Folkways, *Simple Gifts*. As a team, George and Gerry now write and illustrate books for children.

This list could go on and on; there are many others who should be named. Someone, someday, should get together a complete directory of dulcimer players so that we could visit back and forth or write to each other. Here are some names I'd like to see on such a list—and there are, of course, hundreds more! Some of these I intended to present here with statements of their own, but it just was not possible to contact everyone. Others, I have heard much about but have not met as yet.

Tom Kruskal, my co-teacher of dulcimer one year at our Folk Music Week at Pinewoods Camp on Long Pond near Buzzards Bay, Massachusetts, is the best jig- and reel-player I ever saw. He covers the fretboard with a dazzling display of "hammer-ons" and slides to produce almost unbelievable effects.

Then there's Lorraine Lee in the Boston area, Peter McElligott and Dick Wilkie in upstate New York, and, at Pinewoods Camp, a host of my former pupils who should have been teachers (and they are—I for one have learned much from each of them): Myra Elmers, Jan and Kathleen Oosting, Mary Addis and Mary Rhodes, to name but a few.

Tuning and Playing Techniques From Some Dulcimer Friends Around the Country.

In a little while, some friends will be introduced who will tell about their methods of tuning and playing the dulcimer, and how they use it in special situations (playing duets, playing along with other instruments, etc.). As you read their discussions of instrumental technique, in particular that of tuning, you will discover, of course, some overlapping. There are, for example, different ways shown of arriving at the same tunings. This is *not* done to confuse you, although it probably will! Here is the reason. The Appalachian dulcimer has not, up until the present, been in the mainstream of American music (not even American *folk* music as the masses have known it). It has been the property of a few mountain-country people—farmers and hunters—usually unlettered musically, but fine musicians in the classic folk tradition. Naturally, then, there exists no standard written body of instructions.

A person who wanted to learn to "pick the (sic) dulcimore," as my Dad would say, always just picked one up and "fooled around with it." Maybe he would listen to his Dad, sister, aunt or neighbor before he began to play; then he would develop his own style and add fancy touches as time went on.

I feel that the variety of approaches presented here, although perhaps confusing in places, is valuable at this stage in the development of the dulcimer. As we all pool our knowledge until everything possible is learned, standard and "best" methods will emerge. Please bear with us! And bear in mind that most of what we have written and diagrammed and notated and tabulated is really quite simple—it only *looks* complicated on the printed page.

So this chapter is presented with three main purposes in mind: 1) to give the would-be player (we're assuming he or she is not a complete beginner), whether a music teacher or not, enough of a basic understanding of how the instrument works so that he can experiment on his own, 2) to provide some more advanced techniques for the person who must (or thinks he must) depend on music notation, and 3) to bring together in one place, as best we can, the *beginnings* of a vast pool of dulcimer knowledge.

There are some who say, uneasily, that we shouldn't fill this pool; that trained musicians have no business taking over the wild tumbling song of the dulcimer, making it read notes and play Beethoven (let alone Bluegrass music and that unmentionable Rock-and-Roll, modern pop stuff and all). But I say the bubbling mountain spring has long refreshed me and my people before me, and we know that although the pool rise full to overflowing, the untamed spring will always be down there at the bottom of it, renewing the waters.

My Own Basic Tunings— A Review from The Dulcimer Book

Those who are familiar with *The Dulcimer Book*, my dulcimer-for-beginners effort, will remember that tunings were given for each of the six Greek modes, because the dulcimer fretboard is diatonic, like a piano keyboard with no black notes.* Most true folk songs tend to stick to their modes; therefore, the player of folk tunes on the dulcimer never need notice the lack of halftones once he learns how to make the few simple turns of the pegs necessary to get the instrument ready for the song at hand.

For the benefit of those who have not learned the tunings from *The Dulcimer Book* or from one of the other instruction books available (see bibliography), here is a short review of my basic tunings, with a few additions.

In the beginning book, I suggested only one way of tuning into each of the modes, so as not to confuse the reader. There are, of course, variations on those tunings which you will probably find by yourself as you get acquainted with your instrument. I shall give here one variation for each of my basic modal tunings, except for the Lydian and Phrygian, which our music rarely uses. You may learn more of the alternates for each mode from the other people writing (or written about) in this book, or from other publications, the best of which is probably a little self-produced booklet, *Dulcimer Tunings*, by Martha Schecter (see bibliography).

My tunings given here are for four-string dulcimers; however, they may be adapted for the three-string dulcimer by treating the third string (on the three-string dulcimer) as the fourth (on the four-string). That is, on a three-string dulcimer, the bass string is the third.

I number the strings this way: As the instrument lies on your lap, tuning pegs to your left, the string nearest your body is the *first* string, or string #1; the two middle strings are the *second* and *third* (#2 and #3), respectively, and the farthest away is the *fourth* (#4), and is usually the only bass string. These tunings are the ones that work on my own dulcimer, which is strung with three banjo (five-string banjo) seconds and a wound fourth. (Of course, all this is just the reverse for left-handed players!)

I am supposing that you know 1) how to sit and hold the dulcimer, 2) how to use a noter if you wish to, 3) how to do a simple thumb strum (right hand action), 4) how to play the scale and pick out a familiar tune, 5) how to use a feather pick if you want to, and 6) how to do simple fingerpicking. These and other beginning techniques are described in *The Dulcimer Book* (pp 17-20) which, although written for the three-string dulcimer, can be used on a four-string just as well in *The Dulcimer*). When reviewing this information in *The Dulcimer Book*, however, it might be easier, if you do have a four-string dulcimer, to convert it temporarily to a three-string by a simple maneuver. Loosen the second string and move it over along the bridge until it lies very close to the first string, and tune it back up to pitch. You now have a "double" first string; that is, both strings are noted or pressed down as one. *Or*, move the second string over until it lies very near the third string. Now you have a double second string, which some people prefer (especially those of us who, for the most part, only note or make melody changes on the first string). You may wish to take a sharp knife and saw tiny grooves in the bridge for moving the string back and forth, but I sometimes change mine over and let the string just lie on top of the bridge for that song. I do this fairly often when playing a four-string dulcimer in order to get the picking rhythm I want without changing dulcimers.

Now for the tunings.

---

*If your dulcimer has an "extra" fret (between the sixth and seventh frets on a traditionally-fretted dulcimer), ignore it for the space of this lesson. Call it 6-1/2, or 6♯, or 7♭ if you like, but it is not included in my instructions. For an explanation of this fret and how you may find it useful, see p. 64.

How to hold the noter.

Simple thumb strum.

Using the feather pick.

How to Hold the Dulcimer

Jean showing how to sit and hold the dulcimer. "This dulcimer, the latest one designed by my husband George, is slightly more compact than our earlier ones, and is the one we now make for our friends."

The Major Key (Ionian Mode)

Turn the fourth (bass) string up to where the tension is good—don't make it too taut or you may break the string. Now, press down with your finger on this string just to the left of the fourth fret (this is actually the fifth tone above the bass, since the open bass string counts as tone #1 of the scale). Now, with your right thumb, pluck the string. The note you hear is the note to which you will tune the three treble strings (the first, second and third). This done, you are ready to play in the major key. The first note, or *do* of the major scale falls at the third fret on the melody (first) string. You are now tuned to a chord that sounds 1-5-5-5; or do-so-so-so. With notes, the relationship would be a middle C bass, and G-G-G above middle C for the treble.

Major key variation: Press the bass string at the first fret, sound the tone and raise the bass string to the note you have heard; it now sounds a *fourth* below the treble strings, instead of the former *fifth*. Now, tune the first or melody string an octave above the bass. The scale begins, as before, at the third fret. Note: If the pitch is fairly high, above the E above middle C on the bass string, it is better to tune the first string in unison with the bass instead of an octave above; otherwise you risk a broken string. I can tune quite high on my melody string, but each dulcimer is different, and you will soon find the limits for your own strings.

The Minor Key (Aeolian Mode)

To tune from the major key into the minor, press down on the bass string just to the left of the sixth fret and sound the note. Tune only the first string to this note, leaving the other treble strings and the bass as they were in the major tuning. Now, starting from middle C on the bass, the new relationship of your notes is C-G-G-B♭.

Minor key variation: Starting from the above minor tuning, turn the second and third strings an octave above the bass. *Or*, turn only the second

string to the octave, leaving the third to make a fuller chord.

The Mixolydian Mode

Many of our Southern Appalachian songs are in the older modes, especially the Mixolydian and the Dorian. Try *Old Joe Clark* and *Goin' to Boston* in the Mixolydian tuning.

For the Mixolydian tuning, have your bass string at a comfortable pitch, then press down at the third fret, sound the note, and tune your first, second and third strings to that tone. They will be four whole tones above the bass. That is, if your bass is middle C, the treble strings will be F-F-F above. The scale begins on the open melody string (O in the tablature).

Mixolydian variation: If your pitch is fairly high (say D or E), make the third string take the bass note (let's take E), and drop the fourth string down to the octave below the first and second strings. This gives a very satisfying "deep bass" sound to the chord.

The Dorian Mode

The Dorian scale is almost like minor, or Aeolian, except that when one comes to the sixth note in the scale it sounds unexpectedly major.

Tune your bass string to a comfortable pitch, press down the third fret, sound the tone, and tune the first string to this tone. Tune the second and third strings to the tone sounded at the fourth fret on the bass, as you did for the major key tuning. If your bass is C you now have C-G-G-F. The scale beings on the fourth fret.

Dorian variation: Press down on the bass string at the third fret, sound the tone, and tune the second and third strings to this note (the fourth note of the scale). Press the bass at fret six, sound the tone, and tune the first string to the note sounded (the seventh note of the scale).

The Lydian Mode

Note: The Lydian and Phrygian modes are almost nonexistent in American folk music. Since I don't believe you will have much use for them, I will give here only one tuning for each.

The Lydian mode is like the major (Ionian) mode, except that the fourth note of the scale sounds "sharp." To tune to the Lydian mode, turn the bass string to a good pitch and press down at the first fret. Tune the first string to this note. Strings two and three should be tuned to the note found when the bass string is pressed at the fourth fret. The scale now begins way up, on the sixth fret. Let me know if you have any traditional songs that fit this scale. They are scarce!

The Phrygian Mode

Although this mode is not often used nowadays, many mountain tunes sound beautiful when harmonized with it. Tune your bass as usual, but choose a somewhat higher pitch (D or E), since the first string has to drop quite low and might sound "watery" in C. Once the bass is tuned, press down at the fourth fret, sound the tone, and tune the second and third strings to that note (same as major key tuning so far). Now, press down on the *first* string at the second fret, and turn it until it sounds the same as the open second string. You may feel that you need a third hand for this, but it can be done easily if, as you turn the peg with your left hand, you press the string with your (right hand) index finger, and use the thumb to sound the string as you tune.

The "Extra" Fret

Now that you have learned to tune your dulcimer to the six Greek modes, and before our young friends are introduced, I should say something about that "extra" fret that some dulcimers have. Both Holly Tannen and Chuck Klein have instruments equipped with this fret (added in between the sixth and seventh frets on a regularly fretted dulcimer), and they allude to this in their notations. If your dulcimer doesn't have it don't feel bad, for it isn't necessary. It is easy to have one put on, however, if you want it.

Briefly, here is the history of this vagabond fret. Traditional dulcimers, as you know, are fretted diatonically (like a piano keyboard having no black notes). If you start with the open tone (O) on the first string and play up the scale through the seventh fret, you will get a complete Mixolydian scale (G to G—try it on the piano), not the Ionian or major. The major scale begins on the *third* fret, and corresponds to the notes C to C. The Dorian scale (D to D) begins on the fourth fret, the Phrygian (E to E) on the fifth fret, and the Lydian (F to F) on the sixth fret. The "extra" fret most likely came into being because someone did not understand this scale arrangement, and tried to force the beginning scale on the fretboard (beginning with O) to be major. The seventh tone sounded flat, so he put in another fret.

After the extra fret was put in, however, it proved useful because now it was possible to play, beginning at O, tunes in either the Mixolydian or Aeolian scales without retuning, thus allowing more flexibility for players wanting to jam with other instruments when quick tuning is essential.

Now to meet our first two young players. Both of them discuss tunings in a knowledgable way, and perhaps it is a good time to think about *how* different people arrive at the various tunings. Another thing these two have in common is that both have had much experience in playing along with other instruments; so we'll let one follow the other, ladies first.

Holly Tannen:
Playing the Dulcimer
With Other Instruments

I was born and raised in New York City, and in college and graduate school I studied things like psychology, zoology and anthropology. I had some music training and play the piano. I live now in and around Berkeley, California, playing music and working with horses. The two people I play and sing with most often are Janet Smith and Rita Weill, but I also play dulcimer, banjo and piano with a square dance band known as "Colonel Sanders and the Southern Fried Chickens." Since I like to play the dulcimer in groups with other instruments, I'll talk about that aspect of playing.

When I was seventeen I received my first dulcimer as a present from a boyfriend who'd met Jean Ritchie at the Berkeley Folk Festival, became turned on to dulcimers, and learned to make them. I bought Jean's book and taught myself to play. Then I began to pick up tunes from records. For years I was too shy to play in front of even my closest friends. Then, in the fall of 1968, I went to Seattle for the Sky River Rock Festival and met Will Spires and Dr. Humbead's

"New Tranquility String Band." Willie encouraged me to play for them and fiddled along with me on *Goin' to Boston* and *Uncle Joe*. I was overwhelmed. I thought string band music was the most beautiful thing I'd ever heard and determined to learn to play it. I spent the next few months hanging around Berkeley, playing with any old-timey musicians who'd let me join in. Dave and Phyllis Ricker invited me to sit in with their "Contra Costa County Contrapuntal Banjo Band," an informal living room group that met two or three times a week. It was in this setting that I developed a style of playing the dulcimer which allows it to fit in with most any stringed instrument. I don't know how to describe the joy that flows from sitting down with friends and making love to them by playing music together. In this chapter I hope to share with you the skills I've learned from playing with such fine people as ballad singer Rita Weill, mandolin virtuoso Ken Hall, banjo player Ellen Bush (queen of the Silver Lizard banjo) and guitarist Janet Smith.

Preparing Your Instrument

Dulcimers are as individual as their makers—mellow or loud, funky or fancy. You may have to do some work on yours to set it up for speed and ease of playing. If you really love wooden friction pegs for their beauty and authenticity, then keep them. I've replaced mine with geared banjo pegs for faster and more accurate tuning. The strings on wooden instruments change pitch with the temperature, so in the course of an evening all the musicians may have to retune to each other many times. If you decide to replace your pegs, look for banjo or guitar pegs with a high gear ratio; cheap geared pegs are less reliable than friction pegs.

Playing with other instruments is simplest on a dulcimer with three strings tuned to D, D, and D an octave below. I advise my students to remove their fourth string, and, if the three remaining strings are not equidistant, to have new grooves cut in the bridge and nut. I use two silvered steel guitar first strings and a bronze-wound guitar fourth. Two banjo first strings and a wound banjo fourth will also work; if you have a very large dulcimer you may have to get heavier strings and tune lower. Get lots of spare strings—experiment with different gauges—and change them frequently.

If you know a good guitar maker or repairman, you can have him put in an extra fret between your sixth and seventh frets. This will enable you to play a major scale going from the open string to the seventh fret, to play in either major or Mixolydian without retuning, and add interesting trills. Tunes such as Mike Seeger's version of *Don't Let Your Deal Go Down* use both the flatted and the natural seventh that this "6-1/2th" fret gives you.

Carry your dulcimer with you everywhere. You'll run into musicians in the unlikeliest situations. A good hard case is well worth the semi-exorbitant price you'll have to pay for it, but you might want to settle for a quilted cloth bag or a vinyl gun case.

How to Play with Fiddles, Mandolins and Banjos

Most any American or British fiddle tune can be played on a dulcimer. Some, such as *Miss McLeod's Reel (Uncle Joe)* and *Bonaparte's Retreat*, are melodic and essentially chordless. They can be played in the traditional fashion, by fretting the first string and using the other two as drones. Tunes which date back to the nineteenth century, when a dance band consisted of a fiddle and a banjo, are generally structured this way. Around the turn of the century the guitar was introduced into string bands and the shape of tunes began to change, becoming more chordal. You can adapt the dulcimer to these modern tunes by playing chords on it, but you sacrifice the ancient droning bagpipe sound of the instrument in the process.

Latch onto a local fiddler or banjo player. You may have to seek one out since they are sometimes shy. In the meantime, you can practice these techniques on songs from string band records, such as those of the "New Lost City Ramblers."

Fiddlers play primarily in the keys of D, G, and A. Tune your top two strings to the fiddler's D, your bass string an octave below. Mandolins are tuned just like fiddles, and you tune to them in the same way. Banjo players will play in C major or C modal tuning, depending on the song, and will capo up two frets to D; or you can tune your strings down to C. Start out with well-known tunes in D: *Soldier's Joy, Bonaparte's Retreat,*

Mississippi Sawyers, Miss McLeod's Reel, Goin' to Boston, Sourwood Mountain. At first you may have trouble hearing and following the melody, but don't worry about it; not many things you play on a dulcimer can sound *bad*. You can learn a tune either by playing it over and over until it becomes fixed in your mind, or by having your friend play it for you phrase by phrase. As you learn more tunes, you will begin to teach them to your friends in this way.

A tune like *Don't Let Your Deal Go Down* can be played with or without chords. Chords are simpler to play on a dulcimer than on a guitar. A G chord is made by pressing all three strings at the third fret, an A chord by pressing all three strings at the fourth fret. These are the most common chords in the key of D but all the others are played in the same manner—all three fingers across the fret of that name.

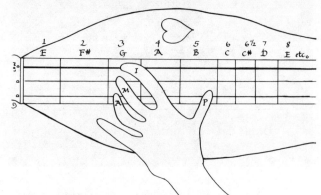

The letter names of the fingers are taken from Spanish guitar terminology.

Play a G chord by pressing the string closest to you at the third fret with the ring (R) finger, and the bass string with the Index (I) finger. Put your thumb down on the first string at the fifth fret to round out the chord. Now move your whole hand up a fret. This is an A chord. If you put your thumb down on the 6th fret, you have A minor; on the "6-1/2th" fret, A major. Experiment moving your hand up and down the fingerboard, hammering on and pulling off with your thumb. You can retain some of the drone sound by playing "half-chords"—lifting up the I finger and chording just the first two strings.

Now you can play along with most fiddle tunes in D. It takes a lot of playing before you can hear chord changes. If there is a banjo player or guitarist in the house, ask him to holler them out for you.

66

Don't Let Your Deal Go Down

Traditional

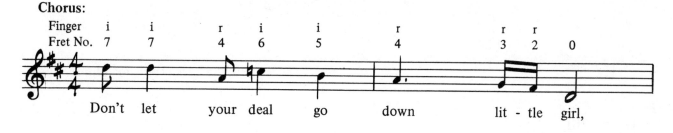

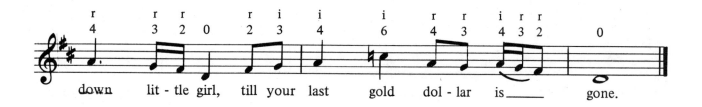

I've been around this whole round world
I just got back today
I've played cards with the king and the queen
The ace, the deuce and the trey.

Chorus:

Who's gonna shoe your pretty little foot
Who's gonna glove your hand
Who's gonna kiss your red ruby lips
Who's gonna be your man?

Chorus:

Papa's gonna shoe my pretty little foot
Mama's gonna glove my hand
Sister will kiss my red ruby lips
I don't need no man.

Chorus:

Where did you get them high-button shoes
Dress that you wear so fine?
I got my shoes from an engineer
And my dress from a driver in the mine.

Chorus:

In the key of G you can't play so much of the melody, but you can provide a rhythmic accompaniment to other instruments and to your voice. Your base position will be the G chord at the third fret. A C chord is played at the sixth fret; a D chord has all the strings open, though you can vary this by putting your A finger down on the second fret or your thumb on the fourth fret.

Irene Goodnight

Huddie Ledbetter and John A. Lomax

The musical notation is for the vocal line only; the dulcimer part is written in tablature above it.
In the (D) chord all the strings are unfretted unless specified.

In the key of A your chords will be D, all strings open, and E, fretted at the first fret. Your right-hand strumming will be the same bom-biddy-bomp that Jean has described in *The Dulcimer Book*—the rhythm of a galloping horse.

As you become familiar with different tunes, try to pick up on and accentuate the rhythmic highlights of each one. Play these with heavy downstrokes (toward you) of the feather: DON'T let your DEAL GO DOWN, LITtle GIRL. I try to follow exactly the rhythm that the fiddler plays, even though my notes may be different from his. It is this touch which makes the dulcimer blend in so well with string bands.

How to Play with Guitars and Autoharps

Most autoharpies play primarily in the keys of C, F, and G. For G tunes you may keep the dulcimer tuned to: D-D-D and play out of the third fret as you did for *Goodnight Irene*. But if your friend has a large repertoire in all three keys, you'd do better to tune all your strings down a whole note to C. Your fretboard now reads like this:

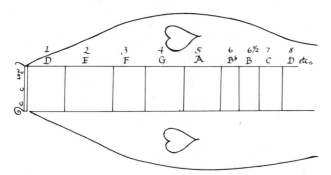

The dulcimer fretboard with all three strings tuned down a whole note to C.

To play in F, play out of the third fret as described for G, above; to play in G, play out of the fourth fret as for the key of A. Autoharp players change chords frequently, sometimes with every note. You don't have to follow all these changes, only the ones that sound important.

Guitarists are fun to play with because they can play in any key to accommodate you. The guitarist can get a good deep bass by tuning his bottom E string to D, for songs such as *The Handsome Cabin Boy*. This tune illustrates another way of fitting the dulcimer to specific tunes—by playing melody lines on the bass string when they go below D.

Guitarists can also experiment with modal tunings such as C tuning, capoed up two frets to put it in D.

There's no limit—except your own imagination —to what and with whom you can play. Thumb your nose at anyone who says, "You can't play *this* music on *that* instrument." I've jammed on Macedonian tunes with *bouzoukee*, Israeli songs and Moroccan belly dances with *oud* and *doumbek*, Italian schmaltz waltzes and Irish jigs and reels with accordians, even flamenco and rock tunes. Just grab the best and most receptive musicians you can find, feed them dinner, sit them down in your living room or backyard, and start picking. That's what folk music is all about.

The Handsome Cabin Boy

Traditional

*5', 4', etc. means to finger these notes on the bass string.

The captain's wife she bein' on board she seemed
   in great joy,
To see her husband had engaged such a handsome
   cabin boy,
And now and then she'd slip him a kiss, and she
   would've liked to toy,
But 'twas the captain found out the secret of the
   handsome cabin boy.

Her cheeks were red and rosy, her hair all
   in a curl,
The sailors often smiled and said, "He looks
   just like a girl,"
But eatin' of the captain's biscuits her color
   did destroy,
And the waist did swell of pretty Nell, the
   handsome cabin boy.

Around the bay of Biscay our gallant ship
   did plow,
Among the sailors there a rose a frightful
   scurryin' row,
They tumbled from their hammocks for their
   sleep it did destroy,
And they cursed about the groanin' of the
   handsome cabin boy.

"Oh Doctor, dearest Doctor," the cabin
   boy did cry,
"My time is come, I am undone, and I must
   surely die,
The doctor come a-runnin' and a-smilin' at
   the fun
To think a sailor lad should have a daughter
   or a son.

Even more additional lyrics to *Handsome
Cabin Boy*

The sailors come a-runnin', they came to gape
   and stare,
The child belonged to none of them, they
   solemnly did swear,
The captain's wife she smiled at him and
   said, "Dear, I wish you joy,
For 'twas either you or I betrayed the
   handsome cabin boy.

Then each man took his tot of rum and drank
   success to trade,
And likewise to the cabin boy who was neither
   man nor maid,
Here's hopin' the wars don't rise again, our
   sailors to destroy,
And here's hopin' for a jolly lot more like
   the handsome cabin boy.

Chuck Klein: How I Tune By Ear

Now, here is Chuck Klein. Like Holly, he is New York City born and raised. I first met him at the Mariposa Festival in Canada in 1971, when he came up from the audience and offered to demonstrate contemporary-style playing during my dulcimer workshop. He was a bronzed young kid with long hair and a polite manner; I took him to be a local Toronto boy. It was not until two years later that I learned that he was neither a kid, nor Canadian, but a successful optometrist in New York City.

Chuck: It seems that the majority of dulcimer players I run into are, like myself, untrained in formal music, Now, by-ear playing is all very well and good when playing alone or with people who know your style, but has drawbacks when sitting down with other musicians. If you have a good ear you can pretty well pick up a song as you play it—if you can get into the right tuning, which is what I shall discuss first.

We'll start with three assumptions: 1) we are using a four-string dulcimer; 2) we have the extra fret, or full seventh note, which is becoming more and more popular; and 3) we have tuning pegs that won't slip!

Here is how the fretboard looks, up to the first octave:

Nut	1		2	3		4		5	6	7	8

I know that this extra freet is being discussed elsewhere (see p. 64), so I won't repeat it here. Some people refer to this fret as "6½" but I refer to it here as #7. For example, the traditional dulcimer scale on the fretboard as I have drawn it (listing the extra fret as #7) is: o-1-3-4-5-6-8. A regular major scale is: 0-1-2-3-4-5-7-8.

Major Tunings

Tuning into the Key of C

When playing alone, the dulcimer can be tuned to whatever pitch sounds best on your instrument, or whatever range you find easiest to sing in. When playing with other people, you need to tune to standard notes, especially when playing with non-tunable instruments like harmonicas, autoharps, pianos and hammer dulcimers. Let us say you are going to play in the key of C. The other musicians will be ready to go, but chances are you'll have to do a bit of tuning. To get to the key of C, tune your strings, beginning with the melody string (the one nearest to you):

C-C-G-C

(On a four-string dulcimer, the last C above will be for the bass string. For a three-string dulcimer, just eliminate that last C; the bass string on the three-string dulcimer will then be tuned to G.)

You get the C note by asking someone else to sound the note for you. Tune your first string in unison to it; then tune the second string to the same pitch. Next, tune the bass (fourth) string to the same note an octave lower. Last, play the bass string at the fourth fret and tune the third string to that note, which is G. Here is the fretboard with the notes that you now have:

To make sure you are correct, these are checks available to you:
1. 4th string at 4th fret = 3rd string open
2. 3rd string at 3rd fret = 2nd string open
3. 4th string at 8th fret = 1st string open
4. 1st string = 2nd string

Tuning into the Key of D

For the key of D, simply turn all the strings one step higher. Your strings now play these notes: D-D-A-D.

Now you have a pattern you can use for other tunings, keeping the same relationship between the strings, as long as the strings do not get so low that they lose their tension. Some dulcimers sound good when tuned low, around the key of G; others sound muddy when tuned down that far, and ring truer up around C. My dulcimer is one of the second type—if I tune to G by tuning to open G-G-D-D, it sounds terrible. How then do I tune to G, or lower, to F?

Open Tuning vs. Third Fret Tuning

Let's refer to the tuning pattern we have just learned where the home tone can be heard by strumming across the open strings without fretting at all, as "open tuning." Now I'll give you another term—"third fret tuning." This means that the key is established when the first string is fretted at the third fret; the resulting chord will contain the tonic, or root, and the scale which proceeds upward from the third fret to the eleventh will be a regular major scale. The seventh fret (the "extra" one, remember?) is counted here but is not played in third fret tunings (unless the tune uses that note!). Of course, if your dulcimer does not have this note, then the top note of the octave will be your tenth fret.

Tuning into the Key of F— Third Fret Tuning

If, starting in C open tuning, you turn the third string down one tone to F you will be tuned: C-C-F-C. Depress the first string at the third fret and strum with the right hand across the strings; you are playing the chord F-C-F-C, which fits in very well with an F chord on other instruments. To illustrate, here is a diagram including three more frets than before:

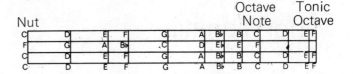

This is how I tune to the key of F. You will hear as you play that the melodies have the third fret as their home tone.*

Tuning into the Key of G— Third Fret Tuning

The key of G uses the pattern D-D-G-D. From the F tuning, simply turn each string up one step. The tonic again is on the third fret. On my dulcimer, this tuning rings out beautifully, while the open tunings for F and G are muddy. All of the different keys may be reached either by open tuning or third fret tuning patterns; which you use should depend on what sounds best on your dulcimer. Or, if you're in danger of breaking a string by one tuning method, switch to the other.

Here is a simple list of the various tunings that may be helpful:

Key	Open Tuning	Third-fret Tuning
G	G-G-D-G	D-D-G-D
A	A-A-E-A	E-E-A-E
B	B-B-F#-B	F#-F#-B-F#
C	C-C-G-C	G-G-C-G
D	D-D-A-D	A-A-D-A
E	E-E-B-E	B-B-E-B
F	F-F-C-F	C-C-F-C

Concentrate first on C, D, and G, as your most-used keys. F is also often used, and A is probably the most common fiddle tuning.

*The bass string here will sound somewhat up-in-the-air, but our ears will tolerate it as not being "wrong;" of course, the longer we use it the "righter" it will sound.—JR

Minor Tunings

Some General Hints

My way of tuning into the minor key is simple and fast. The first string is tuned down one note below the first string. Try it from whatever tuning you're in now. If you're in an open tuning, the scale starts on the first fret; if you're in a third fret tuning, the scale starts on the fourth fret.*

Now, some songs in minor keys sound best with the dulcimer sixth fret, and some sound better with the seventh (extra) fret. If you are in an open minor tuning, you have the choice of either. If you're in a third fret minor tuning, you may use *only* the eighth fret (seventh on a regular dulcimer). The same, of course, is true with major scales, but there seems to be more of a recurring problem with minor key tunes.

A Helpful List of Minor Tunings

Key	Open Minor Tuning	Third-String Minor Tuning
G minor	F-G-D-G	C-D-G-D
A minor	G-A-E-A	D-E-A-E
B minor	A-B-F#-B	E-F#-B-F#
C minor	B♭-C-G-C	F-G-C-G
D minor	C-D-A-D	G-A-D-A
E minor	D-E-B-E	A-B-E-B
F minor	E♭-F-C-F	B♭-C-F-C

The three most commonly played of these are A minor, E minor and D minor. That is because they are the relative minor chords of C, G, and F, respectively. For D minor I use the open tuning, and it is my favorite minor key. For E minor, I have a great conflict—I like the sound of the open tuning, but it's easy to break strings getting into it, and the third fret tuning is a little too low for my instrument.

The opposite is true for A minor. Here the open tuning is low, and the third fret tuning is high. Take your pick. Often, if the whole group is about to start playing a song in E minor, you might suggest that it would go just as well in D minor. I get away with that sometimes. At any rate, you will soon find out by trial and error which tunings are best for you.

*The scale that starts at the fourth fret is actually the Dorian mode scale. It *sounds* minor, and is a lovely tuning; we forgive Chuck this minor error.—JR

74

Richard and Michele Heller:
A Lesson from a Real Teacher

Photo by Suzanne Szasz

Right about now, if you haven't played dulcimer very much, you must be longing for a good old-fashioned, school-type lesson, and Richard and Michele Heller are just the ones you need. First, a few words of introduction.

Richard Heller is a young Bronx man who likes old-time banjo and dulcimer music. He heard dulcimer music first in the early 1950's on what he described as "an old Jean Ritchie record" (there are no such things). He was converted wholeheartedly to the dulcimer in 1966 in North Carolina, where he met Edsel Martin and heard him play.

Richie learned to play in Martin's style but added his own improvisations, of course. He never uses a noter, but chords instead with his left-hand fingers. His right-hand fingers pick the tune; occasionally he uses a flatpick, and sometimes finger-picks.

Michele Heller learned to play from her husband, and they often play and sing together on their courtin' dulcimer. They play traditional and contemporary music. They have written a book on their way of playing, and the following lesson is taken from it.

(Excerpt from NONESUCH AND OTHER LIVING RELATIVES: Four-String Dulcimer Instruction, by Richard and Michele Heller and Marvin Salzberg)

Fingerpicking Melody

Michele and Richard both play guitar and banjo as well as dulcimer, and it is only natural that they find themselves borrowing and modifying finger-picking techniques from the first two and applying them to the latter. The *Streets of Laredo* is a simple example of a melody played in finger-picking style. Before you attempt the actual song, try a couple of finger-picking exercises printed below.

First, tune your dulcimer to a Mixolydian mode as follows:

1. Place your four-string dulcimer on your lap as you normally would when preparing to play.
2. The string closest to your body will be known as the *number one* string; the next is the *number two*; the next is the *number three*, and the string farthest from you is the *number four*.
3. Tune the number four string to a low C, one octave below middle C if you have a pitch pipe, piano or reference instrument. If you have no reference note, then tune the string to a note that sounds good and provides sufficient tension to your fourth string, so as to prevent buzzing.
4. Tune your number three string directly to G, a fifth above low C if you have a reference note. If not, then hold the index finger of your *left hand* on the fourth string just to the *left* of the fourth fret. Tune the third string until it sounds identical to the fretted fourth string.
5. Tune your number two string directly to a middle C, if you again have a reference note or can hear an octave above the fourth string note. If not, then place the index finger of your left hand on the third string just to the left of the third fret. Tune the second string until it sounds identical to the fretted third.
6. Finally, tune the first string until it sounds identical to the *unfretted* second string.
7. Now take a deep breath, check your tuning again as described above, and exhale if it sounds correct. If it doesn't sound correct, exhale anyway and start all over again. You are now in a Mixolydian mode.

75

Now, on to the finger-picking exercises. Finger-picking patterns usually use the thumb (T), index (I), and middle (M) fingers of the right hand (unless you are like David Jones who is left-handed). Try the following pattern which we will term *Pattern A*:

1. Pluck the first string with your thumb (T).
2. Pluck the second string with your index finger (I).
3. Pluck the fourth string with your middle finger (M).

Repeat 1-3 again, again, again, again, and again, until you can't stand it anymore or until it flows smoothly. Written out in tablature it looks like this:

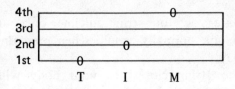

Try this pattern which we will call *Pattern B*:

1. as above
2. plucking the third string with your index finger
3. as above

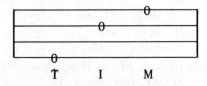

Repeat this pattern a number of times until it flows smoothly. Now for the big test. Try alternating patterns A and B as follows:

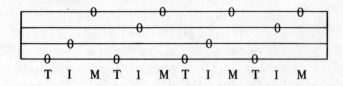

There are other three-finger patterns that you yourself can invent and practice to get the feel of finger-picking the dulcimer. Now, on to the *Streets of Loredo*.

In an attempt to have you fully understand how the song is being played, we have designed a tablature to identify what both left and right hands are doing at any time in the song. At first it will probably be confusing, but we can promise you that a little patience and perseverence will bring you a rewarding experience. Look at this for a moment:

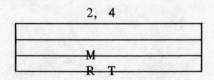

The numbers above the tab tell you what frets are being fingered. The letters tell you what fingers of the *Left Hand* are on strings 1, 2, 3 or 4. For example, the above figure is interpreted as follows. The *M* and *R* fingers of the left hand are on the second fret with the *M* on the second string and the *R* on the first string. The *T* of the left hand is on the fourth fret of the first string. You will note that both the *T* and *R* fret the first string. There is a reason for that and other double-fretted strings in the song. The reason will become obvious as you begin to learn the song. Now look at the following figure for a moment:

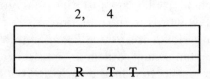

With the exception of Ⓣ, this figure is the same as the previous example. Ⓣ tells you to pluck the first string with the thumb of the *Right Hand*.

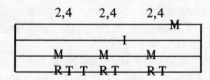

You are now told in the above sequence to hold your *Left Hand* as indicated and to hit the first string with Ⓣ; hit the third string with Ⓘ; and hit the fourth string with Ⓜ of the *Right Hand*. Recognize what your right hand is doing? Right. You are finger-picking *Pattern B*.

Work slowly and carefully keeping in mind that this tablature tells you what your *Right* and *Left* hands are doing together. Look at the next figure for a moment and try to interpret it on your own. Keep in mind that all *Right Hand* tabbed fingers have a circle (O) around them.

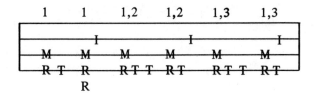

Now check your interpretation with the following. At the beginning your left *M* and *R* fingers are on the first fret with *M* on the second string and *R* on the first string. First, Ⓣ of the *Right* hand hits the first string, followed by Ⓘ of the *Right* hand hitting the third string. Then, while *M* and *R* of the *Left* hand hold their position, *T* of the *Left* hand comes down on the second fret of the first string. Then Ⓣ of the *Right* hand hits the first string and Ⓘ follows by hitting the third string. Finally *M* and *R* of the *Left* hand hold their position while *T* of the *Left* hand moves to the third fret on the first string. Then Ⓣ of the *Right* hand hits the first string followed by Ⓘ of the *Right* hand hitting the third string. Was your interpretation correct? Good. If you didn't fully understand, reread this section from the beginning.

Now you are ready to try the real thing. Musical notation has been provided for those of you who can read music, but is not necessary to learn how to play the song.

Since part of the song repeats itself, you will notice repeat signs ‖: :‖ in the musical notation. Start at the beginning and follow through until you see the repeat sign with the dots to the left :‖ . At that point return to the beginning repeat sign with the dots to the right ‖: and repeat until you see ending 1(⌐1.⌐) marked off. Do not repeat ending 1 but proceed to complete the song with end 2(⌐2.⌐).

Streets Of Laredo

Collected, adapted and arranged by
John A. Lomax and Alan Lomax

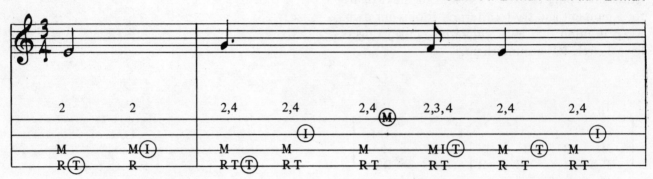

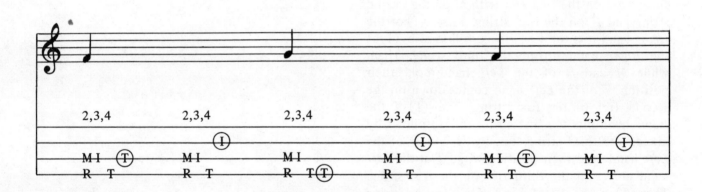

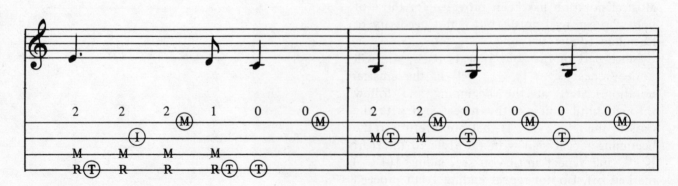

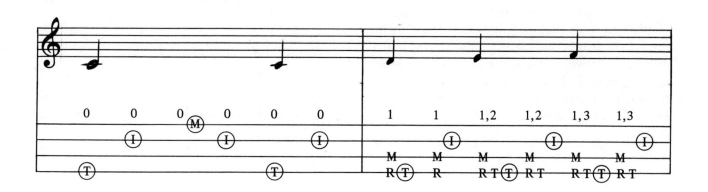

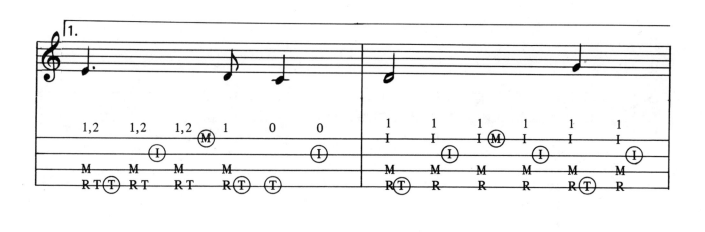

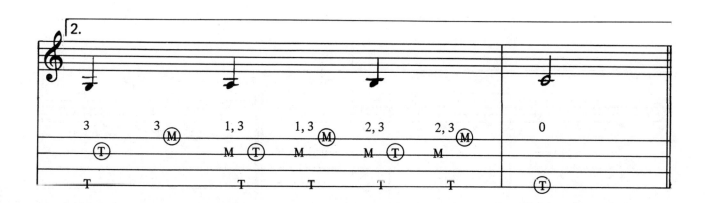

Playing Dulcimer Duets

If you have a friend who plays the dulcimer, then you can play the melody as presented earlier while your friend plays the following accompanying chord pattern. You will find that the second dulcimer will add much to the finger-picking arrangement. This second dulcimer part is played not with picking but with a free-flowing three-four strum. Notice that this second dulcimer part involves one chord pattern moved along the fingerboard. It can be learned quickly enough to teach even the beginning dulcimer player in less than ten minutes.

Streets Of Laredo
(for second dulcimer)

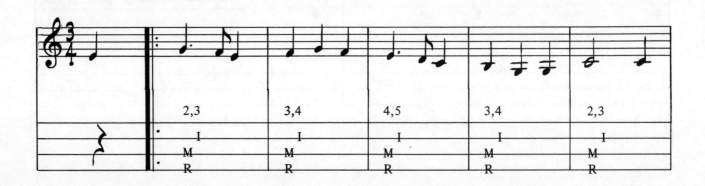

Margaret MacArthur: Thyme for the Dulcimer

Margaret MacArthur of Marlboro, Vermont, is a lovely rosy-cheeked lady with a love for and a definite way with old instruments, especially harps. She was born in Chicago, Illinois, in 1928; her stepfather being a U.S. forester, she lived for varying lengths of time in six other states before her marriage in 1948 to John MacArthur, who shortly thereafter became a physics professor at Marlboro College. Back in 1946, she bought an Austrian zither, and, her interest sparked, soon began acquiring other sorts of old instruments—a harp zither, a flat "breadboard harp," and a fretless banjo among other things. In 1962, John MacArthur, who has a mathematician's understanding of musical instruments, built her a dulcimer. Over the years she has gathered songs, as well as instruments, and is now an important collector and performer of Vermont folk music. She maintains with her husband and five children a warm, welcoming home, bakes the best bread in Vermont, and is New England to the core.

Margaret's handling of the dulcimer is sometimes strong and aggressive, while at other times her touch is so gentle that it is almost non-playing; but her song settings are always tasteful and just right. Of her style, she says, "My dulcimer playing has been greatly influenced by many years of trying to play the Austrian zither. This is especially noticable in the 'hammering on' and 'pulling off' techniques, which are not used by traditional dulcimer players." To illustrate one of her styles, Margaret has tried her hand at tablature to give us this lovely English song, *Thyme*, which she learned from the singing of John Roberts and Tony Barrand, Michael Cooney, and the English brothers team, Robin and Barry Dransfield.

Margaret: Before you attempt *Thyme*, let me give you a brief explanation of my tablature. The fingers of the left hand are designated in the following way: (T) = thumb, (I) = index finger, and (2) = middle finger. The frets to be fingered are indicated by numbers without parentheses. For example,

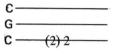

says that the middle finger of the left hand is behind the second fret on the first string,

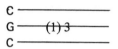

says that the index finger is behind the third fret on the second string, and

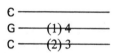

says that the index finger is behind the fourth fret on the second string and the middle finger is behind the third fret on the first string.

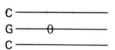

says that the particular string indicated is played open.

The strings can be played individually either with a pick or your fingers. Insert the bass C string in a random pattern wherever it sounds good.

Thyme

As played by Margaret MacArthur

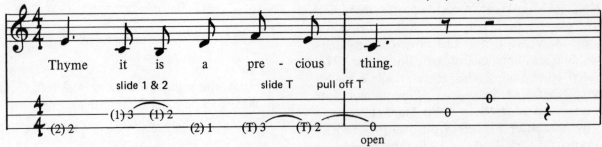

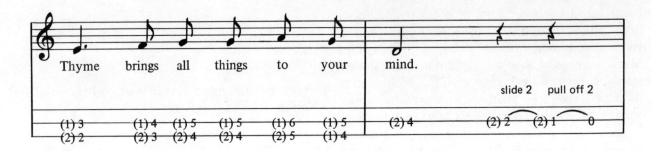

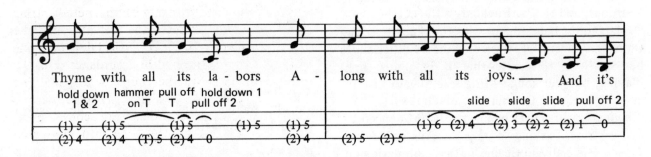

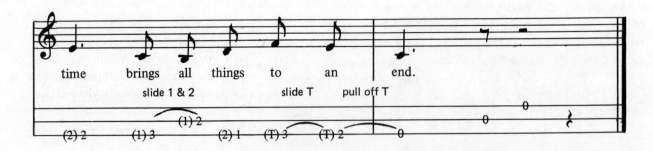

Once I had a sprig of thyme.
I thought it never would decay.
Till a saucy sailor he chanced to come my way,
And he stole my bonny bunch of thyme.

The sailor he gave me a rose.
A rose that never would decay.
He gave it to me to keep me well-minded
Of the night he stole my bonny bunch of thyme.

So all you maidens brisk and fair,
All ye who flourish in your prime,
Beware and take care and keep your garden fair
And let no one steal your bonny bunch of thyme.

Chorus:

Ralph Lee Smith:
An Elizabethan Air

Ralph, a longtime friend of the dulcimer people around the New York area, is now an associate professor in the School of Communications at Howard University in Washington, D.C. He started playing the dulcimer in the early 1960's, and soon developed quite a dazzling technique. He is now planning to publish his own booklet of playing styles. In the meantime, he has contributed the song *Bonny Sweet Robin*, to give us a taste of good things to come.

Bonny Sweet Robin

The Song
This is one of the best-known Elizabethan airs. Print references to it go back to 1583, and it was used as the melody for many different sets of lyrics. Ophelia sings a line of one of these lyrics in her mad scene in *Hamlet*.

Tablature and Playing Style
The melody is played entirely on the melody string, with chording on some of the notes. Ralph uses a hard "French curve" pick to play the song.

In Ralph's tablature, the three horizontal lines represent the three strings, with the melody string at bottom. Dots indicate the fret at which the string is to be played. Three vertical dots on a line indicate a chord, fingered in accordance with the three numbers above the chord. A diagonal line through a note indicates that it is played twice as quickly as the other notes. For convenience, Ralph has divided up the song into numbered phrases.

Dulcimer Recording of *Bonny Sweet Robin*
Ralph plays *Bonnie Sweet Robin* just as it is notated in this tablature on his album, *Dulcimer: Old Time and Traditional Music,* Skyline DD-102. A brochure which accompanies the album gives more information on this song and other songs on the record.

Bonny Sweet Robin

Traditional. Tablature by Ralph Lee Smith

Tuning: do, sol, fa

Dorian

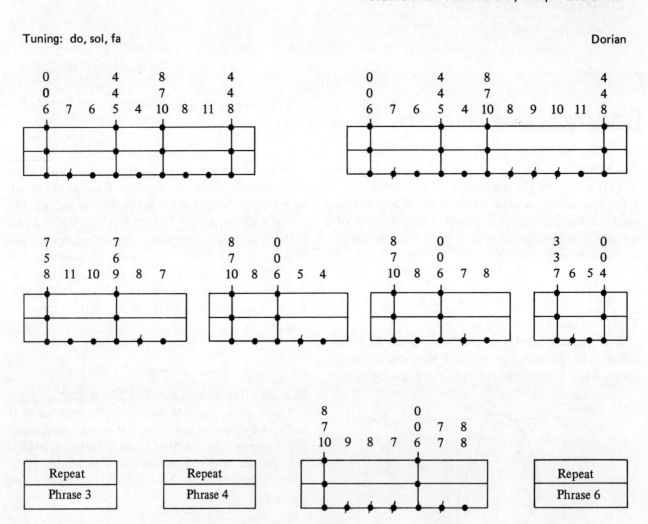

84

Andrew Merritt: The First Dulcimer Virtuoso?

Andrew Lloyd Merritt of Cleveland, Ohio, at the age of seventeen, gives the impression to all who meet him that he excels at everything he does and never settles for less. His dulcimer playing reinforces this impression. Many of us heard his music for the first time at the folk music week in Pinewoods Camp in 1972, and we never tired of hearing and watching him play. And watching is an important part of it, because it is impossible to convey on paper what Andy's technique is like.

The tune he has given us is a traditional one, *Kitchen Girl*, and he has written down the fret numbers to *suggest* the left hand action (which is very nimble since this is a fiddle tune). He strums the strings with his right hand (using a flexible plectrum), with what seems like the speed of light. His elbow and wrist are held fairly high to get an almost breathlessly light touch.

Here are Andy's comments: "As you have observed, my style of playing is an outgrowth of the traditional style of strumming the dulcimer. I just add a few more notes and step up the tempo a bit. I use all the fingers of my left hand (thumb included) to fret the strings, which permits the use of roll-ons, roll-offs, trills, grace notes and such. In order to play both quickly and cleanly it is necessary to develop a light and delicate right hand strum."

"I learn my tunes from fiddlers (notably J. P. Fraley and Lee Triplett) and clawhammer banjo players, and try to incorporate as many of the fiddler's notes as I can with a dulcimer."

So, here is the fiddle tune, *Kitchen Girl*. Try it slowly at first, and then, with the fiddle in mind, work up your speed.

Kitchen Girl

Arrangement by Andrew Lloyd Merritt

Howie Mitchell's Style

One of Howard W. Mitchell's most charming and endearing qualities is that he can always be counted upon not to take himself too seriously. His sense of humor is with him constantly, and what's more, he gets away with it. (I just made a typographical error and tapped out "sense of human. . ." Maybe that's a better way to say it after all!) Everyone always feels relaxed and safe when Howie's around, as though the moment is in good hands.

When I attempt to describe his dulcimer-playing style, I find it hard going because he plays in almost every way that has ever been thought of, and some that haven't been. When I asked him about his playing, I got this answer: "I've done a bit of it all—played for fun, for profit, for Proffitt, singing in tune, out of tune, not at all, using noter, quill, fingers, plucking, bowing, rapping, and occasionally dropping the dulcimer for unplanned and unintended effect."

Howie and Ann Mitchell play dulcimers separately, or together on their "twi-cimer." They play traditional Appalachian tunes, New England songs, Sacred Harp hymns, Bach, Beethoven and Brahms etc. Here Howie gives us his dulcimer setting for *Drink To Me Only With Thine Eyes*:

Howie: A brief explanation of my tablature will be necessary before you attempt to play the song. First, I'm assuming that you have a four-stringed instrument. Tune as follows:

4th: do
3rd: sol
2nd: do'
1st: do'

In order to simplify the tab, I'm going to let you decide on which fingers of the left hand cover the frets indicated. Use common sense and form configurations that are comfortable. The numbers on the lines refer to the fret positions. For example:

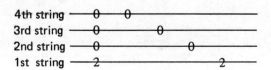

The vertical lines indicate equal-interval beats. With regard to the right hand, the thumb is restricted to the first string, the index finger to the second string, the middle finger to the third string and the ring finger to the fourth string.

This tablature form looks gosh-awful complicated; it's much easier just to play the thing!

Drink To Me Only With Thine Eyes

for 4-string dulcimer

4th: do ————
3rd: sol ————
2nd: do' ————
1st: do' ————

Numbers refer to fret numbers; "0" means open string.

Traditional. Ben Jonson

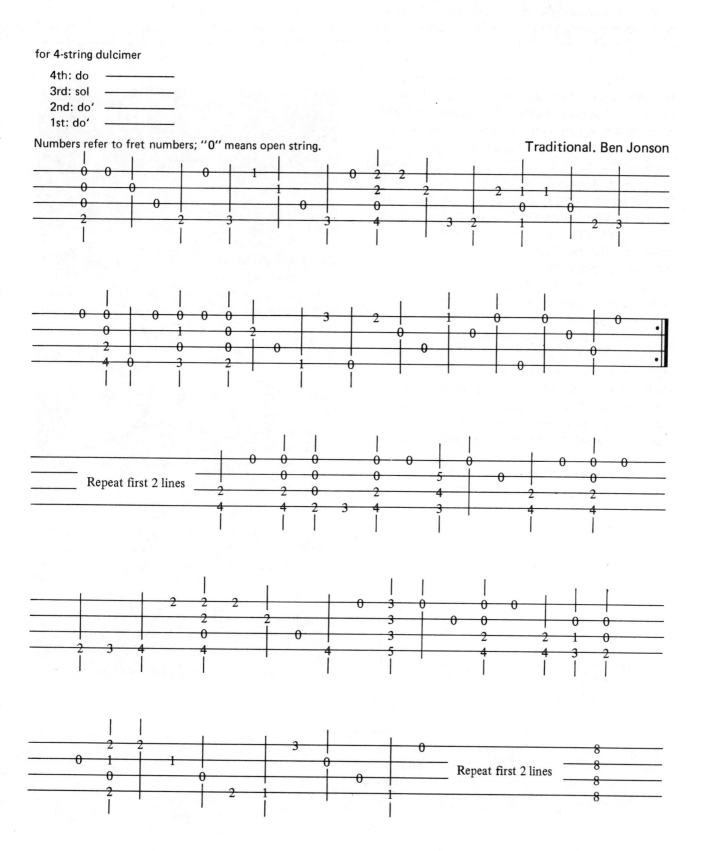

Seven Jean Ritchie Songs
With Suggestions About
Playing Them

As I was writing and thinking about the *scheitholt* a few pages back, it occurred to me that this ensemble or orchestral use of our dulcimers is one we Americans have not developed to any degree. My own dulcimer classes at Pinewoods Camp near Buzzard's Bay (Mass.) each August are about the nearest to ensemble work that I have ever gotten. We sometimes have seventeen or eighteen players, but they learn at varying rates of speed during the week. We have great fun, but we can *not* be called an orchestra!

Lyn Elder, of the Magic Mountain Workshop in Mill Valley, California, tells me of a dulcimer orchestra led by Anne Halvorson, some fifteen players who perform religious music for churches and temples. This would seem to be an American beginning, a realization of the broader capabilities of our dulcimer. My sister Edna and I used to play simple duets with two dulcimers, as do my sons and I at home now; and several loving couples we know, such as George and Gerry Armstrong, Howie and Ann Mitchell, and Richie and Michelle Heller, Edna and Floyd Baker, play the courting dulcimer, or double-dulcimer, or twi-cimer—by any name it's just as sweet. But not many folks of my acquaintance have sat down with three dulcimers and consciously worked out a trio, or four dulcimers, for a quartet.

Of course, some experimenting along these lines has been done, and I'm sure we'll all soon hear of it. I know that many musicians are already beginning to think of grouping together for this purpose. If you are two, or three, or four or more people who want to start ensemble playing, my advice is to start with something familiar, using a fairly simple arrangement.

Let us suppose now that we have four dulcimers, tuned to a major chord, C-G-G-G (bass-middle C, trebles-G above middle C). We'll try a familiar tune, *Amazing Grace*. Our arrangement is based on the old shape-note version. First, here's how the vocal harmonization looks (Sacred Harp Version):

Amazing Grace

John Newton
Dulcimer arrangement by Jean Ritchie

A - maz - ing grace, how sweet the sound, that saved a__ wretch like__ me; I once was lost, but now I'm__ found, was blind, but now I see.

Yes, when this flesh and heart shall fail,
And mortal life shall cease,
I shall possess, within the vail,
A life of joy and peace.

This earth shall soon dissolve like snow,
The sun forbear to shine;
But God, who called me here below
Will be forever mine.

When we've been there ten thousand years,
Bright-shining as the sun;
We've no less days to sing God's priase
Than when we first begun.

Twas grace that taught my heart to fear,
And grace my fear relieved;
How precious did that grace appear
The hour I first believed.

Through many dangers, toils and snares
I have already come;
'Tis grace has brought me safe thus far,
And grace will lead me home.

The Lord has promised good to me,
His word my hope secures;
He will my shield and portion be
As long as life endures.

Amazing Grace

This arrangement is for 3-string dulcimers. To play it on a 4-string dulcimer, move your second string near the first (about 1/8" apart) and treat the two together as the first string. An alternative is to move the second string over near the third and treat those two middle strings as the second string.

Dulcimer arrangement by Peter Pickow

Tune dulcimers G G C
(for 4 string dulcimers—GGGC—treating the first two strings as one)

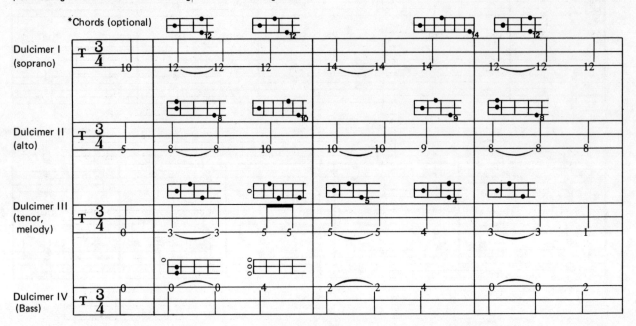

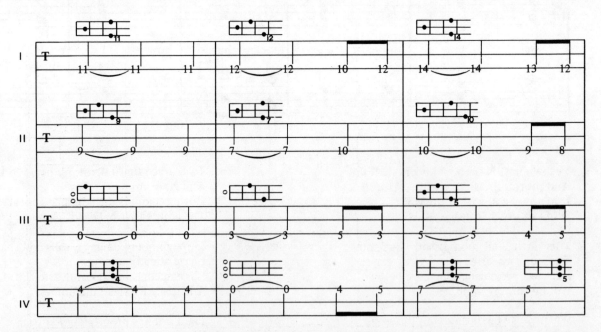

*chord diagram—the three horizontal lines represent the strings of the dulcimer, the vertical lines the frets, the dots your fingers. The small numbers underneath the diagram tell you at which fret the first (melody) string is fretted. An open circle to the left of a string means that that string is not fretted but still plucked. An "x" to the left of a string indicates that that string is not fretted and not plucked. Thus, "⊙⊞⊞⊞" would read "first string fretted at the second fret, second string open and to be sounded, third string fretted at the third fret."

The chords given here with are intended merely to fill out the harmonies created by the notes of the tablature for each of the four parts. These single notes by themselves are sufficient, being transcribed from a sacred harp arrangement of the tune.

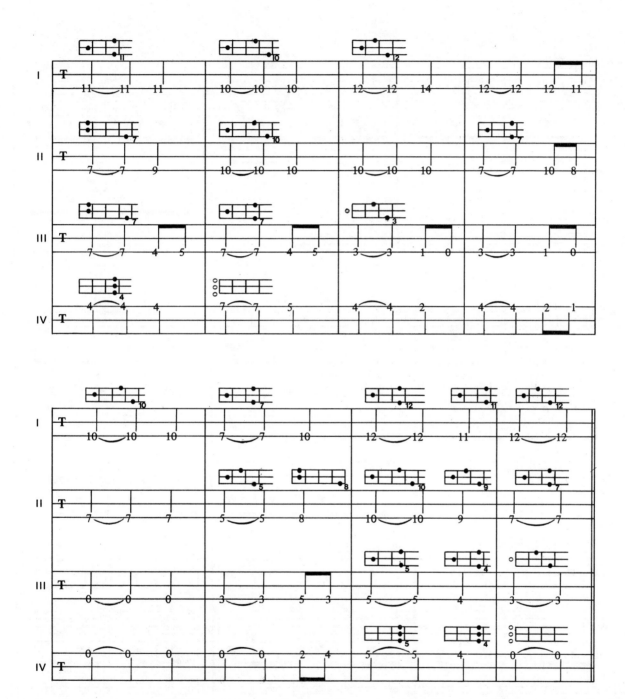

The Peace Round

Our family sings, usually, but Peter is an instrumentalist. Through him, we have discovered the fun of playing rounds on our dulcimers, without always singing, and that's an easy way to get great harmonies without having to read or improvise, since each player just carries the melody in turn. If you like this idea, try *The Peace Round*.

Jean Ritchie

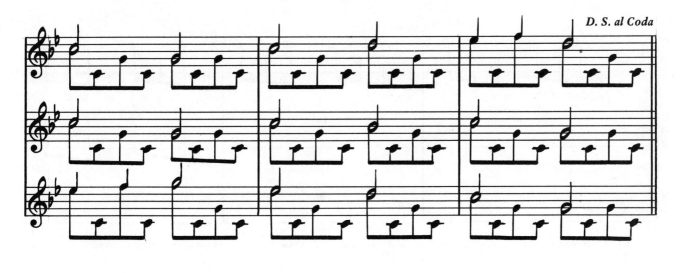

D. S. al Coda

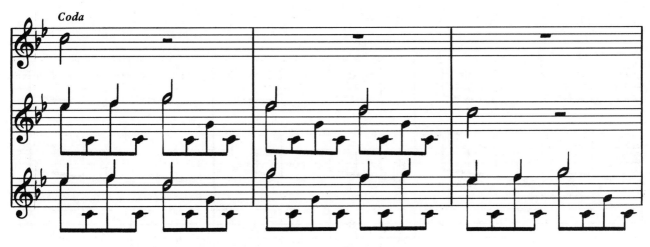

Coda

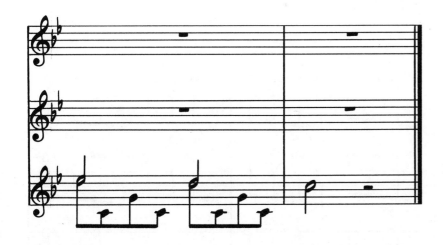

Sing it:
What a good-ly thing
If the chil-dren of all men
Could dwell to-ge-e-ther
I-n peace, O,

A Note About D.S. al Coda

"D.S." is a form of music writers' shorthand. D.S. is an abbreviation of 'Dal Segno', Italian for 'from the sign'. In other words, when you get to this point go back and start at the sign (𝄋) without a break in the music. This has the effect of keeping the piece going in two parts with no ending or beginning. This can be repeated over and over (as long as the company will allow). When you're ready to end it, just observe the second part of the phrase "al Coda" which is Italian for "to the Coda". In other words, play only until you reach the sign "𝄌" and then skip over what's left and pick up (again without a break) where you see the sign "𝄌" repeated down below, above the part marked "CODA" which is a distinct end of a musical piece.

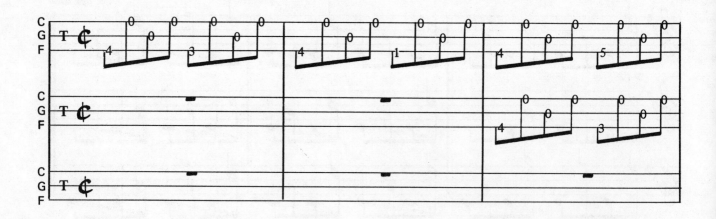

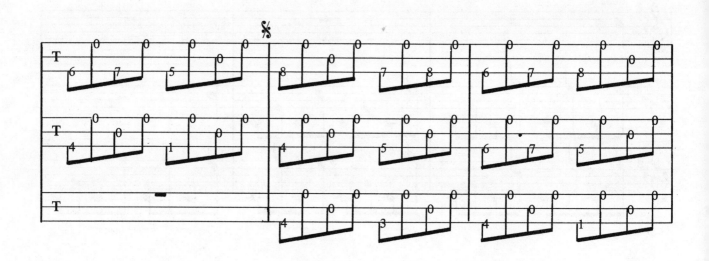

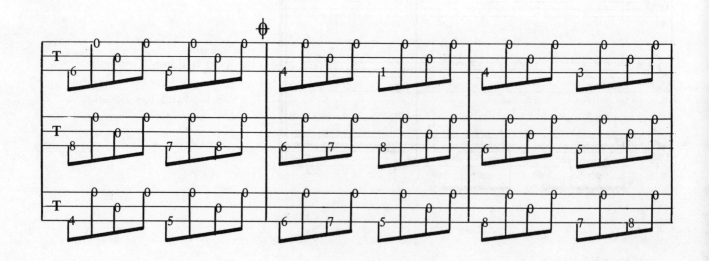

94

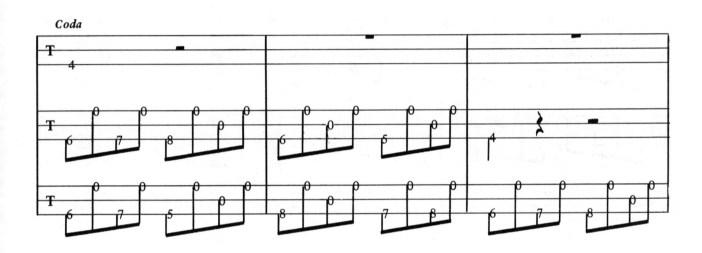

Coda

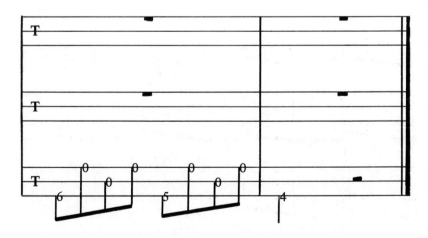

Fair Nottamun Town

Now try a harder round. Here's *Fair Nottamun Town*, played as a two-part round (more parts are possible, but tend to muddy it up and overlap). This is very effective when sung unaccompanied, also, but for now, just play:

Arranged and adapted with
additional lyrics by Jean Ritchie

Tune dulcimer C A A D or 7 5 5 1

Arrows (↓) indicate where other voices enter if tune is played as a round. (Sounds best with 2 or 3 voices.)
Arrows (↑) indicate a brush across all the strings.
Asterisks (*) indicate where additional parts, or voices, may enter when the tune is played as a round.

In fair Nottamun Town, not a soul would look up,
Not a soul would look up, not a soul would look
   down,
Not a soul would look up, not a soul would look
   down
To show me the way to fair Nottamun Town.

I rode a grey horse, a mule-roany mare,
Grey mane and grey tail, a green stripe down her
   back,
Grey mane and grey tail, a green stripe down her
   back,
There wa'nt a hair on her be-what was coal-black.

She stood so still, she threw me to the dirt,
She tore-a my hide and she bruis-ed my shirt.
From saddle to stirrup I mounted again,
And on my ten toes I rode over the plain.

Met the King and the Queen, and a company more,
A-riding behind, and a-marching before.
Came a stark-naked drummer, a-beating a drum,
With his heels in his bosom come marching along.

They laughed and they smiled, not a soul did
   look gay,
They talked all the while, not a word did they
   say;
I bought me a quart to drive gladness away,
And to stifle the dust, for it rained the whole day.

Sat down on a hard, hot, cold-frozen stone,
Ten thousand stood round me, and yet I'us
   alone;
Took my hat in my hand for to keep my head
   warm;
Ten thousand got drown-ded that never was
   born.

Teaching a class (on the mountain dulcimer) at Pinewoods Camp, Buzzards Bay, Mass.

None But One

This is written for one dulcimer. Adapt it, if you wish, for two or three instruments. It's a beauty!

The tune is based on that of *Nonesuch*, an ancient English ritual dance. One day, while playing it on my dulcimer, I was struck in such an especial way with the beauty of the old melody that I began to wish that it had words, so that I could sing as well as play it. To my knowledge there were none, but the tune was hypnotic and as I played more slowly, savoring the tune, these words came. I believe they are true.

Jean Ritchie
Dulcimer Arrangement by Peter Pickow

all of them are | bro thers. And | sound- ing all a- | round a sound, A-

I | mine and I | th- i- ine, Fa-

round and ev ery | where, And | none but one | can un der stand,

ther, mo- ther, son; I | me and I | thee — and

1.
none but one can | hear:

all of us are | one. I

2.
I

I saw four travellers in a dream
All in the wind and weather,
The chain they carried in their hands
It bound them all together.
And one was yellow, one was red
And older than the others,
And one was black and one was white,
And all of them were brothers.

And sounding all around, a sound,
Around and everywhere,
And none but one can understand,
And none but one can hear:
I mine and I thine,
Father, mother, son;
I me and I thee,
And all of us are one.

One I Love

Here's another pretty one, partly old, partly new. It is based on a fragment of an old song from around home, a dim memory from childhood. Not being able to find the song again when I grew up, I added some of my own words to fill it out, a refrain, and the melody that came from the dulcimer to suit the words.

Traditional
Arranged and adapted by Jean Ritchie

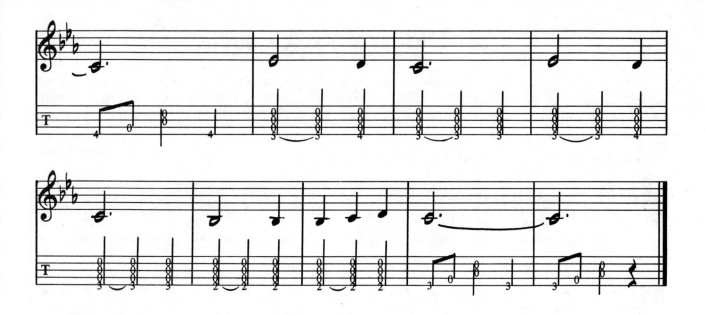

All of my friends fell out with me
Because I kept your company;
But let them say whatever they will,
I love my love with a free good will.

Chorus:

One, I love, two, he loves,
Three, he's true to me.

They tell me he's poor, they tell me he's young,
I tell them all to hold their tongue.
If they could part the sand and the sea,
Then they might part my love and me.

For when the fire to ice will turn
And when the icy sea will burn
And when those rocks will melt in the sun,
My love for you has just begun.

Over the mountains he must go
Because his fortune is so low,
With an aching heart and a troubled mind,
For leaving his love so far behind.

It's when I'm awake I find no rest
Until your head lies on my breast,
And when I'm asleep I'm dreaming of
My one, my dear, my absent love.

Last Old Train's A-Leavin'

This is a gentle, reflective song, so although it's a good dulcimer-picking tune, don't do it too fast, and go a little softly on the picking. It's a sort of lament for all of my people who have had to leave home and the loved mountains to make a living in the cities.

Jean Ritchie

Tune dulcimer 5 5 5 1

Don't you want to go?

Melody break

Standin' on the mountain, standin' on the
  mountain,
Standin' on the mountain, don't you want to go?

Chorus:
O, the last old train's a-leavin', the last old train's
  a-leavin',
The last old train's a-leavin', don't you want to go?

Hear the hills a-falling, hear the hills a-falling,
Hear the hills a-falling, don't you want to go?
Hear the nightbirds calling, hear the nightbirds
  calling,
Hear the nightbirds calling, I don't want to go!

See the timber burning, see the timber burning,
See the timber burning, don't you want to go?
See my newground turning, see my newground
  turning,
See my newground turning, I don't want to go!

See the people going, see the people going,
See the people going, don't you want to go?
See my redbuds glowing, see my redbuds glowing,
See my redbuds glowing, I don't want to go!

Standin' on the mountain, standin' on the
  mountain,
Standin' on the mountain, don't you want to go?

What'll I Do With This Baby-O

A fine example of putting ditty-words to a dance tune. Women minding the sleepy young 'uns in the back room at a Saturday night party would make up words to whatever tune the fiddles and banjoes were playing in the next room. There are hundreds of verses, naturally; those given here are some traditional ones and some I made up when my own children were small.

Jean Ritchie

Tune dulcimer A A A D or 5 5 5 1

What'll I do with this baby-O (etc.)
Wrap him up in a tablecloth,
Wrap him up in a tablecloth,
Throw him up in the fodder-loft.

What'll I do (etc.)
Tell your daddy when he comes home,
Tell your daddy when he comes home,
Tell your daddy when he comes home
And I'll give Old Blue your chicken bone.

What'll I do (etc.)
Pull her toes, tickle her chin
Pull her toes and tickle her chin,
Pull her toes, tickle her chin,
Roll her up in the countypin.*

What'll I do (etc.)
Dance him north, dance him south,
Dance him north and dance him south,
Dance him north, dance him south,
Pour a little moonshine in his mouth.

What'll I do (etc.)
Every time the baby cries,
Stick my finger in the baby'e eye!
That's what I'll do with the baby-O,
That's what I'll do with the baby-O.

*Counterpane

The Ritchie's cornfield cabin. (About one mile from the house.) Used for eating dinner during workdays and for sleeping overnight on hunting trips.

Hank Levin:
How To Make An
Appalachian Dulcimer

Every dulcimer maker gets asked over and over, "How do I go about making a dulcimer?" or, "Can you send me a set of plans?" or, "Could I come to your shop and apprentice until I learn how to make my own dulcimer?" Some even have the nerve to write, "I'm doing my thesis on folk music. Would you please send me a complete list of books and records on Appalachian songs and tell me how to make a dulcimer?"

Well, I always feel bad, not being able to sit down and draw up a set of plans for each of the hundreds of people who've asked me those questions, but somehow we never had the time even to write it out just once and have it printed—we always meant to, but life gives each of us just so much time and no more, and the other things at hand always had to be done first. Then came the time when Uncle Morris Pickow passed away, and without his help, we didn't even have the time to make our dulcimers anymore. We tried to answer the letters that continued to come, or redirect them to other craftsmen, but still they continued to pour in to us.

One day in the late fall of 1971, a car pulled up to our door in Port Washington, and a young family got out of it, and came in to see us. It was Hank, Lynn and Robin Levin; we had never known of them before. Hank handed me one of his dulcimers, in a lovely blue-velvet quilted bag, saying that this was a gift of appreciation for having "turned so many folks on to dulcimers. A small crumb of all the bread you have cast upon the waters!" We were very much moved by such a thought, and by such a family, and we liked Hank's craftsmanship and his way with the instrument. We built a fire, and had some supper, and before the evening was over, we had asked the Levins if they would consider making dulcimers for us, through their workshop on St. Marks Place in New York, Musical Traditions. Hank thought that this idea would be a good boost for his business, which, like almost everyone else's, needed a boost about that time. We gave him our design, and have been well pleased with the results. In fact, Hank has never disappointed us in anything, and he was our natural choice as the author for our "How-to-Build" section. We are sure that you won't be disappointed, either.

Dulcimer Construction

Hank: It's fun to build a dulcimer, and really something that anyone should be able to do. Experience in woodworking is useful, but the primary requirement is the love of the dulcimer. Some ability to play, or at least a deep appreciation of the dulcimer and her music will provide far more incentive than superficial cabinetmaking skills. My good friend Dharmendra Jadeja, an Indian prince from Gujerat, built many of the instruments in use in the United States today, and he had no professional knowledge of woodworking before building dulcimers!

Tools

The beginner may be amazed at how *few* tools are absolutely essential for building a dulcimer. Don't hesitate to begin with whatever tools might be lying around the house. Go to the library and get a book on basic carpentry and become familiar with what tools are available for what jobs. Buy economy versions of these tools only as you really feel that they are necessary. Imported tools are available so cheaply that it pays to try them out and use them until they fall apart. Then after building several dulcimers, if you decide to replace them with expensive high-quality tools, your familiarity and experience will help you to make a wiser purchase.

Incidently, I would be embarrassed to show a professional cabinetmaker some of the scraps of metal which have become important parts of our dulcimer production!

Here is a small list of tools you will probably end up with before you're done: a coping saw with an assortment of blades (unnecessary if you're lucky enough to have access to a jigsaw); a big, course half-round file (¾" or 1" bastard); a fine flat mill file for dressing the frets when the instrument is done (check for flatness at the hardware store with a small steel rule—most are flat on one side, but many are flat on neither); a tapered reamer for pegs (unless you use tuning machines); a cabinetmaker's scraper (you *must* find out how to sharpen and use this from a book on carpentry); sandpaper in the following grades—80, 100, 150, 180, 200, 400; and a container of Franklin's *Titebond* glue.

The only tools above that are *absolutely* essential are the coping saw, files, and whatever grades of sandpaper you can scrounge, and of course the glue.

Dulcimer Styles and Basic Parts of the Dulcimer

First I'm going to explain the types of dulcimers in use and the basic characteristics of construction in each. Then I'll lay out a procedure through which you'll be sure of completing your dulcimer. I'll also throw in some valuable pointers which should save you lots of time and money and enable you to turn out surprisingly competent work.

By dividing the dulcimer into three sections and treating each section separately you will get a better understanding of the different styles of dulcimers. There are actually only a couple of types of heads, the same of bodies, and even fewer of fingerboards. Obviously, we will then easily understand the many possible combinations of the three.

Fingerboards

First let's look at fingerboards. Most are 3/4" high by 1-1/4" wide. If you have other preferences based on experience or observation, fine. But if not, these are safe proportions. The fingerboard is rectangular with a "plucking hollow" cut or sanded into the top surface anywhere between the 15th fret and the bridge. The length of the fingerboard (and to some extent the length of the body of the instrument) is determined by the "vibrating length" of the strings; i.e., the distance between the nut and the bridge. The exact placement of the frets is also determined by this distance, and I will say more about that below.

The fingerboard gives a better sound when it is hollowed out, which must be done before the frets are put in, but this is not essential on your first dulcimer. The top surface of the fingerboard must be planed perfectly flat. It may be best to have a carpenter do this on a joiner.

Fingerboard cross-sections

a) Easiest   b) Preferred   c) Glued (not as easy as it looks)

There are several traditional ways of placing the bridge at the lower end of the fingerboard. I've found the best sound to result from a saddle being set into a notch cut into the top of the fingerboard to receive it. A less desirable variation would be to simply place a prism-shaped bridge on the surface of the uncut fingerboard; but it will be found that if this is not glued into place, it can be expected to shift constantly and throw the fingerboard out of tune. The least preferable style is nevertheless quite common. As illustrated, the tail-cap is extended up slightly above the top surface of the fingerboard at its very end. It is rounded into a sort of bridge, and notched to hold the strings. Apart from being non-replaceable, it hampers the sound by transmitting the strings' vibrations directly to the most solid and least resonant part of the body—right into the tail block! For this last style of "bridge," the fingerboard and the body must be designed to end at the correct bridge distance from the nut to maintain the validity of the fret spacings.

Kinds of bridges

Inlaid into fingerboard

Resting on fingerboard

Tailcap acting as bridge

The nut, which supports the strings above the fingerboard at the head end, is nearly always fit into a groove in the fingerboard as described above for the first (and preferred) kind of saddle. This groove should be just at the joint between the fingerboard and the head. It can be made of hardwood, such as rosewood, or of bone, ivory, or plastic. I generally set it into a notch about 1/8" deep, and take care that it fits quite well into the notch all the way across the fingerboard, and seats all the way to the bottom of the notch. It should extend about 3/32" above the surface of the fingerboard. Later, after the dulcimer is finished, this nut will be notched to space the strings correctly and hold them just barely above the height of the frets.

Similarly, the bridge should be set into a notch about 1/8" deep, and should extend above the fingerboard about 1/4". It will also be notched with the same string spacings as the nut, but it will hold the strings up to a height of 5/32" above the fifteenth fret when measured at that fret.

Finally we come to the location and inlaying of frets. It is worth noting that dulcimers, as well as many guitars, are seldom in tune with themselves. This is not difficult to detect for an accomplished musician listening to the instrument played solo, but it becomes painfully obvious to nearly anybody who hears the dulcimer played in concert with another instrument. This defect is always caused by reliance on any one of a number of "folk" techniques for locating fret placement. (The most commonly recommended error is to divide the distance between nut and bridge by eighteen, subtract the result from the total length, divide again, etc.; then, for the dulcimer, utilize the second, fourth, fifth, seventh, etc. steps to ascertain the correct locations of the dulcimer's frets. When this is done, it will be found that the octave fret does not fall halfway between the nut and bridge as it theoretically should, and is evidenced in the simplest test for intonation—the octaves are out of tune! To cover this up, makers who out of ignorance persist in using the above method will usually hide the defect by correcting the octave fret and letting the mistake fall somewhere else. This is common on inexpensive Spanish-made guitars as well as dulcimers.)

Correct fret placement is made in reference to a formula found in most musical engineering textbooks, and according to this formula, I have provided a fingerboard layout correct for a calculated *theoretical* scale of 28-3/4". Note that the bridge is actually located .08" further from the center of the seventh (octave) fret than is the nut. This corrects the tendency of the strings to be stretched into sounding sharp when they are pressed down to the frets. The distance from the fret side of the nut to the fret side of the bridge must therefore measure exactly 28.83".

Fingerboard fret scale layout for 28¾" scale.

Distance from "nut" to 1st fret = 3.13 inches
Distance from "nut" to 2nd fret = 5.92 inches
Distance from "nut" to 3rd fret = 7.21 inches
Distance from "nut" to 4th fret = 9.57 inches
Distance from "nut" to 5th fret = 11.64 inches
Distance from "nut" to 6th fret = 12.62 inches
              (optional) 6th fret = 13.51 inches
Distance from "nut" to 7th fret = 14.38 inches
Distance from "nut" to 8th fret = 15.96 inches
Distance from "nut" to 9th fret = 17.34 inches
Distance from "nut" to 10th fret = 17.97 inches
Distance from "nut" to 11th fret = 19.15 inches
Distance from "nut" to 12th fret = 20.21 inches
Distance from "nut" to 13th fret = 20.67 inches
Distance from "nut" to 14th fret = 21.56 inches
Distance from "nut" to 15th fret = 22.34 inches
Bridge saddle = 28.83 inches*

*28.75" + .08" correction—see text.

If you plan to make several dulcimers, you will want to lay these measurements out on the edge of a piece of smooth white cardboard, or even a strip of metal (I use the back surface of cheap aluminum yardsticks) and transfer the markings carefully onto the joined top surface of your fingerboard using a hard sharp pencil. You will need to buy a wooden drafting ruler which has a scale measuring 1/50th of an inch. When measuring, each 1/50th" mark will equal .02". (You are more likely to find such a ruler at a drafting supply shop or large art supply store than in a hardware store.)

Incidently, if you feel intimidated by the complexity of laying out the fingerboard, these spacings have been already laid out in the full-size plans supplied with my kits.

When the correct positions of the nut, bridge, and frets have been marked lightly but accurately,

use a sharp metal point (like an ice pick) to scribe lines perpendicularly across the fingerboard with the aid of a carpenter's try square. The fingerboard is now ready to receive the frets.*

Fretting the Fingerboard

Frets are made either in the form of staples, or employing tanged fret-wire. The staple technique is quite traditional, but was customarily limited to fretting only under the melody string, with the frets running down the side of the instrument held nearest the player. Of course, such an instrument has the built-in restriction that the melody can never be played on the bass string, which can be a beautiful special effect; and chords are out of the question. Most dulcimers today are made with frets which extend all the way across the neck, and are made of a special wire which has a cross section like the letter "T." This can be procured in sufficient quantities for dulcimers from many guitar repair shops. Those who sell dulcimer kits generally supply fret-wire with the kits. Try to get the kind which has been straightened by the manufacturer.

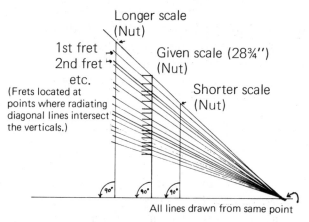

How to get longer or shorter fingerboard scales from the given (28¾") scale.

*If you want to make your dulcimer longer or shorter, lay out the measurements I've given you on a large sheet of heavy paper along a straight vertical line. Then draw a horizontal base line across the end of that measured vertical. Now choose a point on the horizontal line as far as possible from the vertical, and from this point draw lines to the fret locations on the vertical, but extending these lines beyond the vertical if the new scale is to be longer. Now by drawing other vertical lines perpendicular to the base line you can get any size fingerboard and it will be proportionately correct and in tune.

If you prefer to use the staples, you can try using a heavy staple gun (sometimes you can rent them), but they are quite difficult to align accurately. At best you will end up with an amateurish-looking job. The traditional technique was to locate the ends of each staple, generally from 1/8" in from the edge nearest the player, and about 5/8" further in for the other end. Then these positions were marked with a punch and drilled with a drill slightly smaller than the wire the staples were to be made of. Then the staples themselves were made out of thin bailing wire or long thin nails 1/16" or less in thickness. These handmade staples were then carefully tapped into their holes.

Frets are actually no more trouble than this, provided you have a saw blade of the correct width to make the correct size slot, and providing you practice thoroughly on scraps of wood similar in size and material to your actual fingerboard. The saw blade is actually quite critical. If the curf (path cut by the saw blade) is too wide. The frets, of course, will not stay in place—especially through the filing operations which follow. If the curf is too narrow, either the frets will not go in at all, or they will seriously distort the fingerboard or even cause it to be smashed in the effort. I recommend that you purchase a selection of different metal-cutting blades for your little coping saw and try them out on your piece of scrap "fingerboard" before you purchase one of the expensive little dovetail saws supplied by some of the people who sell the fret-wire supposedly for this purpose. I have never found any of them to work as well as some of the small hacksaw blades made for small cheap coping saws.

Practice cutting slots into your scrap of fingerboard wood until you are confident of your ability to cut a slot straight across the fingerboard to an even depth of slightly over 1/16", *without* wobbling and causing the ends of the cut to be wider than at the center. This may take at least a dozen tries, probably more. When you have cut a number of practice slots, cut off a few lengths of fret-wire with wire cutters so that it measures 1/8" longer than the width of the fingerboard, and practice tapping in the frets. Use a hammer, and start by holding the fret up at one end with the other end's tang in the slot. Begin tapping from the end that's down, very lightly at first. This should get the fret started. Then continue to tap the fret in all the way across. There should be a 1/16" overhang on each side of the fingerboard. Learn to put them in carefully so that the top is touching the surface of the wood all the way along the fret—that's the hardest part. Gentle tapping should be necessary. When you've done a few of these, take a fine mill file and practice filing down the ends of your "practice frets" until you can do it without marring the wood or accidently plunking them out. When you feel confident with the above operation, clamp your fingerboard near the edge of your worktable and proceed to saw the slots as neatly as you can. Then put the frets in.

When finished, go back over the frets and make sure none of them has been shaken out by pounding the others. Now file the frets flush with the sides of the fingerboard, and slightly round off the ends of the frets removing sharp corners and jagged edges. Remember that most players find it objectionable to feel the frets' ends sticking out from the fingerboard.

Head Designs

The simplest dulcimer head is really just an extension of the fingerboard about five or six inches beyond the nut. Pilot holes are first drilled from the side for the pegs or machines (usually 1/4" diameter, but check this if you've decided to use machines). Then the peg well is formed by drilling a series of overlapping 3/4" holes down the exact center and the inside is finally cleaned out with a coarse file and sanded. The head is left in this condition until the dulcimer has been entirely finished, then the pilot holes are either reamed out to receive the pegs, or the machines are attached.

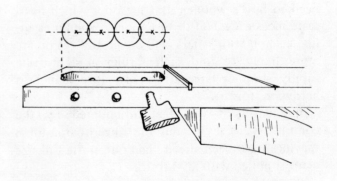

Simple head as extension of fingerboard

A more traditional and graceful head resembles that of a viola. You can leave a plain knob on the end, a blank viola scroll shape (quite traditional), or carve a full viola scroll into it or even the head of Beethoven! The shape is roughly that in the drawing below. First the design is drawn on a block of wood. The pilot holes are drilled for the pegs, then the peg well is drilled out (much as in the simpler head described above). The head is then placed on its side and clamped overhanging the edge of the worktable (or preferably in a vise) and cut out with a coping saw with a coarse blade. If you are lucky enough to have access to a jig or band saw, these will still leave the head rough enough for plenty of fussing.

Scroll-type head (including head-block)

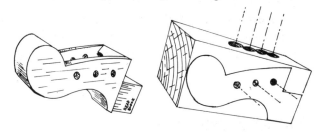

Note that this style head incorporates the head block for the dulcimer's sound box. (See the section on "Body Types.") The exact shape and size of this block sticking out of the back of the head will be dictated somewhat by the style of body chosen. Also, as this head is built into the dulcimer from the start, it must be pretty well finished before the dulcimer is begun.

Machines vs. Pegs

I like pegs. They look nice. And if they are well-fitted, they can be smooth and easy to work. However, this is a slow, careful, and somewhat skilled job—and after fitting pegs on a few dulcimers you'll really appreciate the precision, machine-like fit of the pegs on a fine violin or cello. Still, even with these jewels of classical

sophistication, many folks never get the hang of pegs and commonly resort to "fine tuning" devices. So if you choose tuning machines for your first dulcimer, I certainly won't consider it a "cop-out"!

The trick with pegs is to have the friction balanced on both parts of the peg where it contacts the wood of the head. Use a scraper to make the final adjustment on the peg, as sandpaper is too difficult to control. When the peg looks right, put it in the hole and turn it. If it does not work smoothly, or if it grabs only on one end and not the other, pull out the peg, examine it, and find the shiny spot. Scrape it slightly at this spot and try it again until the friction seems even all the way around. Soap and chalk are very effective for giving exactly the desired balance of smooth turning and "grab" to hold the tension of the strings without slipping, if used sparingly. (Commercially prepared violin peg-dope is seldom more than soap and chalk melted together, and lacks the convenience of being adjustable toward either extreme.)

Certain tools can be used to make the job of fitting pegs somewhat easier. One of these would be a tapered reamer, available at many hardware stores. Get one with a gentle (not abrupt) taper. Work very lightly to widen out the pilot hole, or the teeth will dig in and you'll get a star-shaped hole! A special reamer (expensive) which prevents this by having the teeth milled only on one side, the other side being left smooth, is available from violin maker's supply houses.

Peg shavers are also available at violin supply houses, or they can be made to match your reamer and minimize the work of seating the pegs. They work on the principle of a simple pencil sharpener. But they are so much trouble to adjust that I recommend one only if you plan to make quantities of dulcimers with pegs.

When all is said and done, if you can seat three or four pegs by whatever method and end up with all the pegs sticking out the same length, you can be quite proud of yourself!

If you prefer to use machines, there are basically two kinds recommended. One is the simple friction machine used in ukeleles. The other is the kind of geared tuning machine made for guitars and made with each machine separate rather than in groups of three. Get your machines before you cut out the head, as the design may have to be modified to accommodate the machines—particularly the geared type.

Body Types

The most obvious distinction between dulcimers is found in the body. There are several traditional shapes, and some are many times more difficult to build than others.

First of all, let's look at the basic construction of all dulcimer bodies. There is the top or face, the bottom or back, the sides, the head block (sometimes combined with the head itself, but an important body part), a tail block, and usually a tail cap.

They are generally assembled thus: The sides (known as "ribs") are glued to the head block at one end and the tail block at the other. Then while the ribs are somehow held in position, either the top—with the fingerboard attached—or the bottom is glued into place along one edge of the ribs and onto the head and tail blocks. Then with the position of the ribs secured by being glued to one surface (top or bottom), the remaining surface is glued into place. Later a tail cap is usually glued over the tail block to cover the complex of joints otherwise seen from the back end. Occasionally, as described under "Fingerboards," this extends up and becomes a "bridge". The final step for some makers is to attach the head, although I recommend that this be built into the instrument to avoid the necessity of a complex joint.

Exploded view of dulcimer's parts

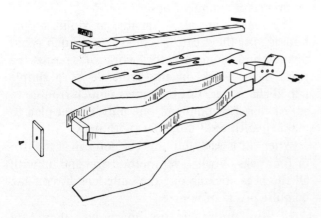

Faces and Backs

Traditional face shapes are shown in the drawing below grouped in order of their complexity. Actually, any shape is fairly easy to cut out with your coping saw; the only increase in difficulty comes from the fact that the face shape determines the amount of work required for the ribs.

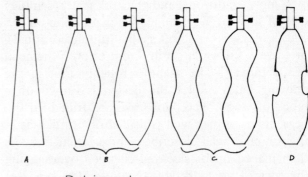

Dulcimer shapes

If you are unfamiliar with woodwork, you may want to try Style A, as you will have enough challenges.

Styles B and C are the most traditional. Style D is illustrated only because it is used by some modern makers. I myself do not find it attractive on a dulcimer (but thats just *my* consideration), nor do I believe it enhances the sound. The construction is similar to that of a violin, and if you do like its looks, you may get a book on violin construction and use it as an advanced project.

My own preference is for Style C, the most usual shape for the Appalachian dulcimer.

The thickness of the back and face should be about 1/10th". I do not recommend the use of the rib "lining" used in guitars to increase the gluing area between the face and ribs, as I have found that the faces and backs glue quite well to the edges of the ribs themselves, and the sound is better without the lining.

I also recommend no bracing, though you may experiment with cross braces at the wide points of the back. The only bracing needed for the top is a good, light, full length fingerboard. I have not found that the sound is improved by modifications of the fingerboard to "make the face vibrate more freely", i.e., partial fingerboards that don't run full length, arched fingerboards (cut out underneath like a Roman aquaduct), or "floating" fingerboards in which the face is somehow disconnected or left unglued at the bridge end of the dulcimer. A certain amount of rigidity (*not* heaviness) is necessary to amplify the characteristic sound of the dulcimer with its rich upper partials (brilliance) more so than in a guitar. By the way, I'm not impressed with dulcimers that sound like guitars!

Soundholes are mainly decorative, and round holes made with a large drill serve fine. Also, one can make a circle of tiny holes for each "sound-hole". But I prefer the traditional heart-shaped holes. They're not so hard to make if you drill two overlapping holes for the lobes, cut the point in with a coping saw blade and finish with a small file or emery board as in the drawing below.

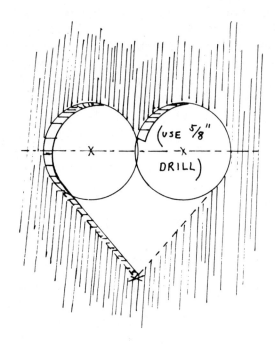

Heart-shaped sound hole

Noting that Morris Pickow used to cut long openings in the face which vented into the hollow fingerboards on the old Jean Ritchie dulcimers (p. 9 in *The Dulcimer Book* by Jean Ritchie), I built several dozen instruments of the same wood to check the value of this procedure. I found consistently that the hollow fingerboard with center holes was significantly better in sound than the hollow fingerboard without holes, and all the above dulcimers sounded better than those of the same design made with solid fingerboards. These central cutouts can be just a row of 3/4" holes up the center of the face, or the actual cutout can be made by drilling 3/4" holes at the ends of the cutouts, then removing the areas in between them with a coping saw.

Center-holes in faces
(Under hollow fingerboards only)

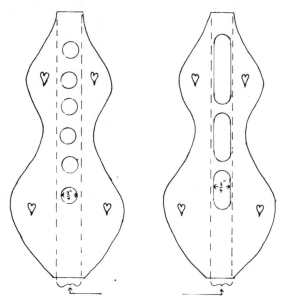

(Area covered by fingerboards)

There is a procedure that is rather difficult to perform which, however, does improve the sound of the dulcimer. This consists of graduating the thickness of the soundboard from 1/10" at the fingerboard to 1/16" at the outer edge. If the graduation is done along a "bell shaped curve", that's even better. This technique is long known to violin and guitar makers, as well as loud-speaker manufacturers. It is often done using a deep-throated micrometer (prohibitively expensive) but is effective if only done roughly with a straightedge as shown in the drawing below. Do not go thinner than 1/16", for the sake of strength; and don't leave an overhang as it could be easily broken off. This procedure is mentioned because it is recognized as a fine point of stringed instrument construction. However, it is not recommended for rank beginners because the musical improvements to the sound will not be noticeable unless the rest of the workmanship in the dulcimer is meticulous—and the consumption of time added to the risk of ruining materials could not be justified.

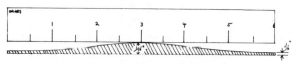

Cross-section of graduated soundboard (not to scale) against a straightedge.

Ribs of the Dulcimer

The ribs, or sides, of dulcimers range from about 1" to 3" in height in the extremes. When measuring a dulcimer, remember that the actual rib height is less than the total combination of rib plus top and bottom thicknesses.

If the sides of the dulcimer are straight, as in style A, you need not pay much attention to the thickness of the ribs, as long as it is in the vicinity of 1/8". However, if the ribs are to be curved or bent, they should be carefully scraped and/or sanded to between 5/64" and 3/32". Over 3/32" in thickness, the ribs become difficult to bend without cracking. If the ribs are unevenly sanded, and must be bent where there is a thick or thin spot, the thin spot will bend first (perhaps quite suddenly) while the heat and steam has not yet penetrated the thick spots and made them supple. This is sure to result in either cracked or broken ribs, or at least flat spots in a curve, where they were not intended.

Rib Bending

Ribs must be bent for two reasons—firstly, so that they will fit into the mold prior to gluing without being made to crack; and secondly, so that after the back has been glued, and the mold is removed, the ribs will not spring back so much that they distort the dulcimers shape while the face is pressed into place for gluing, resulting in a misshapen body.

Bending is fun and really much easier than most guitar and dulcimer making books make it out to be. I use an electric jig which puts out constant heat and distributes it evenly, but this is expensive or at least difficult to build. In the drawing below I have diagrammed a bending jib which you can make at a nominal expense, and is fine for occasional use.

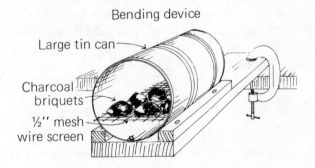

Bending device

Large tin can

Charcoal briquets

½" mesh wire screen

It is true that some skill is required, but once you are familiar with good heat-bending technique—perhaps only after your first dulcimer—you will wonder at the expensive, complicated extremes people think necessary for bending dulcimer and guitar ribs: "curfling" the ribs out of a solid massive hunk of wood by cutting parallel curved lines on a band saw (giving a very weak rib whose fibers are not parallel, very rough, and hard to smooth out); the use of boiling troughs; expensive, heated, full-size presses; or heavy, expensive, unchangeable molds!

The gluing mold, as described in the next section, should be assembled before bending, as it will be needed to test the curve of the ribs as you go along. The exact center of each bend should be determined by holding the rib up to the mold, or otherwise from the full-size plans. The center-points are marked on the *convex* side of each bend with a piece of chalk, to serve as a guide in bending. You will find that corrections can be made later as you are bending, but the positions of these marks should be as accurate as possible.

Clamp the iron to a table as pictured, and when it is good and hot, take an old, thin towel, soak it with water, wring it out, and drop it down over the cylinder in a single thickness. (The metal should be hot enough to that drops of water bounce off it before they evaporate.) While everything is hissing and steaming, take the rib in one hand and a block of wood in the other. First, lightly press the rib with the block (the towel-covered cylinder on the side of the rib which is to be the *outside* of the bend) and rock it back and forth so that the rib is evenly heated over as large an area as possible. Don't try to bend the rib yet—you're just warming the wrong side of the wood so it won't splinter. Now shift the towel slightly so it begins to steam again, and flip the rib over so that the chalk mark is now up and visible. Keep this chalk mark in the center of the area you heat, but rock the wood back and forth against the iron (so that the rib does not suddenly bend sharply in one spot) and when the rib begins to feel quite flexible, bear down slightly. In this manner, continue to bend until the curvature seems slightly less than required for the mold. The block is used in one hand so that pressure may be applied quite close to the hot cylinder itself, if necessary, without burning your hand.

Hank Levin using a bending jib.

When bending ribs to be used in the mold arrangement I describe below (and with most other mold systems as well) the object is not to bend every curve so that it conforms perfectly to the mold before it is put into the mold, but rather to *underbend* so that light forcing into the mold will produce perfect curves under slight tension. This makes the job of bending much less critical, and the curvature will be held in place as soon as the face of the dulcimer has been glued into place. (This tension, built into the instrument, is soon lost as the ribs take a "set.") If you overbend, on the other hand, a bump will stick out when the rib is put into the mold, and this must be carefully bent back using the same technique.

By the way, you will find that different woods have different bending characteristics. The harder the wood, the easier it bends, providing there are no serious irregularities in the grain. Some woods are hard, yet have so little spring action that they need almost no heat-bending—like birch, for instance.

It is of utmost importance that you have spare pieces of the same material as the ribs, and practice using the bending setup until you feel really good about it. I consider this essential enough to include an extra piece of rib material (a "spare-rib", as it were) in my own kits.

Assembling the Dulcimer on a Variable-Shape Mold

Most guitar and dulcimer makers use a heavy, solid outside or inside mold to maintain the shape of the instrument while it is being glued. While this may have advantages in quantity production, it is expensive and time-consuming and not at all justified for one-time (or even occasional) dulcimer assembly. Furthermore, it requires that a different mold be made for every change in size or shape designed into your latest instrument. The drawing below shows a mold-press design which can be assembled at a minimal cost, and which can be altered into totally different shapes by relocating the spindles and clamping tabs.

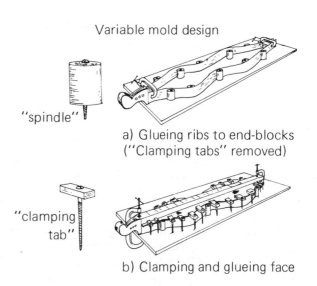

Variable mold design

"spindle"

a) Glueing ribs to end-blocks ("Clamping tabs" removed)

"clamping tab"

b) Clamping and glueing face

To use this mold, simply draw the outline of the dulcimer on the board, cover the board with wax paper, and locate a spindle on the concave side of every bend in the ribs. Long, straight sections of ribs having no bends should have a spindle on each side of the rib to keep it erect when pressure is being applied to the top edge during the face-gluing.

When these spindles have been arranged, partially bend a rib and force it into the mold. If the shape is not satisfactory, change the position of the spindles to produce the desired shape. In my kits, which contain this mold press, I've included full-size plans showing the exact spindle locations for several dulcimer styles, as well as a slightly more detailed description of the gluing procedure; however, the following will give you a very good idea of what is involved.

When the rib shape is satisfactory, the head-block (or the head itself, if the block is part of it) and tail-block are placed in their positions on this mold, and the ribs are glued and clamped to the end-blocks. Any overhang at the ends of the ribs can be trimmed off later.

Meanwhile, the fingerboard should be glued to the face—down the exact center, against a *flat* tabletop, and any excess glue carefully removed by scraping, and sanding when dry. (Drafting tape can be used to mask the areas adjacent to the glue joint, to ease the cleaning job. It is available at art supply stores, and is similar to masking tape but does not have such a tendency to pull up wood fibers when removed.)

When the glue on the ribs and blocks is dry, lightly sand the top surface of each end-block to be sure it is not higher than the ribs, or an ugly gap will remain. Then lightly, with a razor blade, scrape the top edge of the ribs to remove any paraffin that might have gotten on them from the wax paper.

Locate the clamping tabs about every inch or so around the dulcimer, and screw them into place. Turn the tabs away from the ribs, and screw down far enough so there will be minimum resistance when the glue has been applied and speed is essential; now unscrew them back up far enough so that there's room enough to swing the cleats around over the ribs *plus* the face.

Now glue is applied to the top of each end-block, and to the top edge of each rib, as well as to the inside of the face where it will touch the ribs and blocks. Large clamps are used to clamp the fingerboard and face to each end-block, being careful to keep the fingerboard centered on the end-blocks. Then the clamp-tabs are quickly turned in and tightened down over the edges of the face with a screwdriver, pressing the edges of the face to the ribs.

The glued parts are allowed to dry, then the clamping tabs are thoroughly loosened by backing out the screws, and turning back the tabs. The incomplete box is lifted off the mold and set aside for only a moment. (If the partially glued box is stored in this condition, it will lose its shape due to the instability of the ribs. The back should be glued up immediately.)

Now the spindles are removed from the mold. The bottom edges of the ribs are lightly scraped to rid them of paraffin from the wax paper, and the exposed end-blocks are sanded level with the bottom edges of the ribs if necessary. Glue is applied to the ribs, the exposed surfaces of the end-blocks, and to the corresponding surfaces on the inside of the dulcimer back. The back is dropped into the mold between the clamping tabs, inside (glued side) up, centered; now the dulcimer is lowered into place, glued edges down, onto the back and centered carefully. Again the clamps are applied to the fingerboard ends, over the end-blocks, this time to apply pressure to the new glue joint between the back and the blocks. Then the clamping cleats are again turned in and screwed down onto the face, providing pressure which goes down through the ribs to the back. the ribs to the back.

The box is then allowed to dry thoroughly under pressure. When ready, the box is removed from the mold and scraped clean of large drops of glue. The extra length of the ribs and fingerboard should be carefully trimmed down, and, if you like, a tail cap glued over the internal tail-block and fingerboard end, and sanded down to blend with the shape of the body and fingerboard at that end.

The overhanging face and back edges can be sanded carefully down to the ribs with coarse sandpaper *or* an overhang of 1/8" can be left as on a violin, sanding carefully and evenly until it is smooth and round all the way around the dulcimer on both the face and back. At the head and tail the overhangs (if you keep them) can be sanded in to merge with the vertical surfaces of the ribs to eliminate projecting corners.

Sanding

Now the dulcimer is ready for a thorough sanding. Use 80 grade cabinet paper as you would a file, to clean off sawmarks and gross irregularities. The deep scratches it leaves must be sanded out in turn with grade 100. Then the whole instrument is sanded lightly with 100 grade paper until it is free of irregularities, smoothed with 150 grade, and finally just before finishing (and after washing and drying your hands) sanded with 200 grade cabinet paper.

Hold the dulcimer up to the light at different angles in order to spot the glitter of overlooked glue. Thoroughly remove any you find, and re-sand with the finest grade of sandpaper.

Finishing

Finishing of plucked instruments is an extensive, fascinating subject which can be gone into only briefly here. There are, however, two misconceptions which amateur and professional musicians cling to because of lack of opportunity to experiment and observe.

The first is that raw oil of any kind has any place at all in the fibers of a stringed instrument. Oils or waxes soaking into an instrument have a similar effect on the sound to that of a damp washrag.

The other misconception is that a thick, glossy finish can add to the tone. A thick finish, while it provides a high gloss and, to some extent, certain mechanical protection (which average Americans find so important in nearly all manufactured items), almost invariably cuts out some of the sound. Violin technology is actually the source of the fixed idea in the west that heavy finish is tolerable or even desireable. The gloss finish on a violin is actually intended to cut down or "mellow" the excessive treble which is made possible by the continuous imparting of energy from the bow. Plucked instruments, on the other hand, receive their energy for only an instant, and make it sustain as long as possible.*

The "oil-rubbed wood" finish, so attractive in furniture, is actually sought for its quality of permitting the admirer to experience the texture of the exposed wood grain while protecting the wood from dirt and moisture. A similar textural effect is best obtained on a dulcimer by allowing a minimal amount of some brittle finish (such as lacquer or shellac) to soak into the surface of the wood only enough to "seal" it from dirt and moisture. This is wiped on and off before it has a chance to harden into a gloss, and then rubbed with steel wool after it has dried. The result will be an "oil-rubbed" effect with the least possible damage to the brilliance and resonance of your dulcimer's tone.

The best material for this process is either brushing lacquer (a lacquer whose drying time is chemically prolonged to permit brushing), or plain old fashioned nitrocellulose—not acrylic—lacquer from a paint and lacquer company which has been thinned (reduced) according to the manufacturer's recommendation, and enough *retarder* (available at the same place as the lacquer) added so that there's time to brush the lacquer onto a large area of raw wood and wipe it off while it is still wet.

Test your mixture, and the procedure, on a piece of smooth scrap wood before you douse your dulcimer. Be sure you can wipe the wet lacquer off before it has dried enough to bog down the wiping-off rag, which should be a clean cotton rag, free of lint.

After the lacquer has hardened overnight, lightly rub down the entire instrument with 000 or 0000 steel wool to achieve a soft, even luster, carefully working between the frets and in the corners. If you rub through the finish into the wood, simply wipe the steel wool particles carefully off, reapply more of the lacquer as above, and rub it down again.

---

*In much of the world, however, this effect of finish on plucked instruments is acknowledged, and at least the soundboards of the Arabic *oud, saz,* and other instruments is left unfinished. Also, there is a technique used in both East and West (called "french polishing" in English) with which a gloss which is fragile and unsubstantial can be raised with a minute amount of shellac. However, this is a difficult procedure to describe, arduous to learn, and difficult to procure materials for, so I'll not go into it here.

Final Set-Up

Now is the time to attach and adjust the machines, or pegs, in the head. Also, a tail pin or a brass nail or a wooden peg should be inserted in some strong part of the tail, well down from the top surface of the fingerboard. (Be sure to drill a pilot hole for any nail, very slightly smaller than the nail itself, lest it split the wood it is driven into!)

The frets are filed with a fine, flat mill file, just enough so that the file has touched every fret to insure that they are level with one another. Then the frets are lightly sanded with 400 "wet or dry" sandpaper (used dry) to remove the file marks—being careful not to cut into the fingerboard wood)—and the metal particles cleaned out from between the frets with a damp cloth, which will not hurt the wood if it has been properly finished.

Work Neatly!

Don't do things to your wood which will mar it. Don't handle it with oily hands. Don't get drops of water on it—water discolors many woods.

Don't drop the wood—this can cause cracks which may not be noticed until it is too difficult to fix them.

Don't put your assembled dulcimers down on pebbles, or on loose grit from heavy sandpaper, or on the pliers or what have you.

Do a "dry run" on every gluing operation—practice assembling the parts and clamping them without glue so there are no surprises at the critical moment.

Fill any gaps or gouges or similar mistakes with wood putty before finishing the dulcimer—they just might never be noticed!

But you'd better leave a *few* mistakes in your dulcimer, or it might not look like a real folk instrument!

A Word about Kits

You'll notice in the following program for constructing a dulcimer that I've been quite conscientious in giving you the most efficient and straightforward ways to go about building a dulcimer from scratch. You'll also notice, however, that an impressive proportion of time, money, and effort goes into locating the services and cooperation of woodworkers and merchants who are not always understanding—let alone economical—regarding the requirements of an amateur or even small-scale professional dulcimer maker.

Therefore, the purchase of a kit—provided that it is well designed with good quality materials—is justified if it reduces or eliminates the expense, time, and research of strictly commercial nature. Then the builder is left with the actual craft, and esthetic parts, of dulcimer making.

Beware of kits that use ultra-cheap materials such as plywood. The economy involved is rarely reflected in the price of the kit. Also be sure that if a mold is needed, it is provided for in the kit. The guidline I have used in assembling my own kits has been not to ask the amateur craftsman to perform any feat which I as a professional would consider a needless risk of materials, when standard machine procedures are available! This includes a band-sawn head, a joined (machined-flat) fingerboard, ribs sanded evenly to exactly 3/32", faces and backs precision sanded to 1/10", and some of the heavy drilling and dadoing (hollowing out) of fingerboards. I've even found it expedient to include the press-mold and bending jig described previously.

Heaven knows there's enough to do even then to build a dulcimer!

Program For Making A Dulcimer

How to Use the Program

Now with what I've shown you, you should really be able to take any dulcimer you've seen, analyze its construction, and go and copy it—perhaps with your own improvements! This should be far more rewarding than just "following instructions."

But to make sure you don't get bogged down, I'm going to give you a program for building a dulcimer. (Or better yet, a couple of dulcimers—keep the best one for yourself!) Here's how to use this program—and if you leave out any of these three things, well, I bet you'll just never make a dulcimer.

1. Be sure there are *no words in this article you do not understand!* This is very important, because, if you proceed on this project in spite of misunderstood words, you're bound to become discouraged or "lose interest".
2. Know the program thoroughly before you begin!
3. *Start!*

The Program

1. Decide to build a dulcimer.
2. Find out who will cut up your wood *before* you buy it. Know how thick his table saw will cut through hardwood. (If no carpenter in your area can help you, you may be restricted to available veneers or plywood.) Ask him to recommend a source for hardwood. Maybe he's got some odd pieces he'd be glad to get rid of. (Lumber yards often resent selling hardwood for only one instrument, and even plywood must be bought in large sheets, so buying scraps from a carpenter can be quite an advantage.)
3. Decide on a shape and style. Do lots of rough drawings. Decide on machines or pegs.
4. Make good, accurate drawings. Make drawings of each part. Don't forget internal parts—head and tail blocks. *Do good drawings and the dulcimer will put itself together!*
5. Measure the dimensions of each part off your drawings. Make up a parts list with dimension sizes in inches.
6. Make heavy paper patterns of all non-rectangular parts. Symmetrical parts like faces are drawn one side only on folded paper, cut out, and opened out with the fold down the middle. (Remember that faces should be cut slightly oversize and trimmed down on the assembled dulcimer—it's best to make special oversize patterns for the roughcut faces and backs, *and* exact size patterns for finished faces to be used in laying out the mold.) Locate soundhole and fingerboard positions on the patterns, as you may find you can fit a pattern on to pieces of wood you'd have otherwise discarded.
7. Take your patterns and list of part sizes and go shopping for wood. Don't forget material for the bridge and nut (hard maple, ebony, rosewood, or even a piece of bone you can get at a pet shop).
8. Get machines or pegs. You can make pegs, but you can buy viola pegs and you'll have less trouble with them. If you get machines, check to see if they're workable with your design.
9. Have the wood cut to dimension (rectangular) sizes. Include a piece of plywood for the mold. If your carpenter has a band or jig saw, trace the face and head patterns on the correct pieces of wood, and have him cut these out. (Otherwise, you must do it with the coping saw.)
10. Drill out the pilot holes in the block which will form the head; drill out the holes which form the peg-well. Clean up the head, and cut the head-block at its base to the correct angles to receive the ribs.
11. Carefully prepare the fingerboard as covered under *Fingerboards* in this section.
12. Put in the frets as described, and cut the slots for the nut and saddle. Cut, file, and sand the strumming hollow in the fingerboard.

13. Cut out the top. Cut the soundholes and, if you like, the center vents in the top.
14. Glue the finished fingerboard to the top against a perfectly flat surface.
15. Make the body of the dulcimer, as described in the sections on ribs and bodies and mold technique. Do a "dry" assembly before applying glue.
16. Clean the glue off the assembled dulcimer. Do all the trimming, and the rough and fine sanding.
17. Now the instrument is essentially done, but its appearance will be determined by the actions from here on out. Do all the touching up with plastic wood. Put in the nut and bridge.
18. Finish the dulcimer as described, and rub with steel wool.
19. Fit all hardware. Drill pilot hole for tail pin and put into place. File the frets and sand as described in *Final Setup*, and clean fingerboard.
20. String 'er up! Experiment with different pitches to see where your dulcimer sounds best. If you sing, and must have a specific pitch for accompaniment, you may want to try different string combinations to see what gives you the fullest sound at your pitch.

Let me know how you make out!

Where To Buy

Appalachian (Plucked) Dulcimers

This is of course a partial list, limited by 1) my own lack of knowledge, since new makers are starting every day, all around the world, 2) the decision not to include those who have made two or three dulcimers just for fun, or for themselves and friends and who do not wish to go into business on a larger scale, 3) respect for the wishes of those who, like Howard Mitchell, no longer want to be listed as suppliers.

My apologies then to all the perhaps hundreds of good dulcimer makers whom I haven't mentioned here. If you are a dulcimer maker who would *like* to be on this list, send your name, address and particulars to me, and hopefully soon there'll be a revision of this book!

A listing here does not constitute in any way a personal recommendation, by the author or the publisher, of the quality of service or craftsmanship to be had from these people and/or shops. This will have to be determined, as will also the prices, terms, etc. of each, by your individual correspondence with the builders of your choice.

Individuals and/or Shops Offering Dulcimers for Sale

Acme Music c/o Lynn Bagley, 1200 Spring St., Santa Rosa, Cal. 95404

Alpine Dulcimer Co., Box 566, Boulder, Col. 80302

American Dream, The, 4705 College Ave., San Diego, Cal. 92115

Apollonio, Nick, Box 221 Main St., Rockport, Me. 04856

Appalachian Dulcimer Corp. 232 W. Frederick St., Staunton, Va.

Autorino, Michael Rt. 2, W. Searsville Rd., Montgomery, N.Y. 12549

Beall, Jerrold R. See *Farkleberry Farm*

Brewer, George F. 300 Islington Rd., Auburndale, Mass. 02166

Capritaurus Dulcimers P.O. Box 153, Felton, Cal. 95018

Childs, Courtney 789 Maher Rd., Watsonville, Cal. 95076

Cohen, Nuriel, Lieb-Dayan Street No. 1 Meah-Shearim, Jerusalem, Israel

Daniellson, Jim 655 E. 32nd Ave., Eugene, Oregon 97405

Davis, Bill Gatlinburg, Tenn.

Dickson, Reverend Gordon Montauk Highway, E. Moriches, N.Y. 11940. Also teaches dulcimer construction, by appointment.

Dixon, Judge Whitesburg, Kentucky

Dorogi, Dennis Ellicott Rd., Brockton, N.Y. 14716

Dulcimer Shoppe, The 620 E. Broadway, Forrest City, Ark. 72335

Dulcimer Works, The 1723 W. Washington Blvd., Venice, Cal. 90291

Elder, Lyn See, Magic Mountain Workshop

Elder Workshop, Lyn Industrial Center Bldg. Annex, Gate 5 Rd., Sausalito, Cal. Rebecs, hurdy-gurdies, psalteries, lutes and other old instruments.

Farkleberry Farm Rt. 1, Swans Rd., Newark, Ohio 43055

Field, Dave 237 Lexington Ave., Pitman, N.J. 08071

Glenn, Clifford and Leonard Rt. 2, Banner Elk, N.C. 28604

Gonzales, Joseph 529 Indian Hill Blvd., Claremont, Cal. 91711

Harmon, Bob Blowing Rock, N.C.

Hauser, Scott See Live Wood

Here, Inc. 410 Cedar Ave., Minneapolis, Minn. 55404

Hicks, Stanley Sugar Grove, N.C.

Hines, Chet 9760 E. Hasket Lane, Dayton, Ohio 45424

Hughes, Virgil 8665 W. 13th Ave., Denver, Col. 80215

Jeffreys, A. W. See: Appalachian Dulcimer Corp.

Jones, Bill See, Alpine Dulcimer Co.

Kardos, Andrew R. 6605 So. 85th St., Ralston, Nebr. 68127

Kearney, Tam 199 Erskine Ave., Toronto, Canada

Kelischek, George Brasstown, N.C. 28902

Kimball, Dean R.R.1, Box 127A, Yellow Springs, Ohio 45387

Kinsolving, Pitt 7 Silk St., Norwalk, Conn. 06850

Ledford, Homer 125 Sunset Heights, Winchester, Kentucky 40391

Levin, Hank See Musical Traditions

Live Wood P.O. Box 50, Fall Creek, Oregon 97438

MacEachron, Len and Su See Here, Inc.

*Magic Mountain Workshop Box 614, Mill Valley, Cal. *94941

Martin, Edsel Box 367, Swannannoa, N.C. 28778

Martindale, Howard Dean Rd. Hudson Falls, N.Y. 12839

McNaught, Al See, Seedpod

McSpadden, Lynn See, The Dulcimer Shoppe

Meades, Jim Ripley Rd., Spencer, W. Va.

Melton, Raymond Rt. 1, Box 2ll, Woodlawn, Va. 24381

Mitchell, Bill Down East Dulcimers

Muelrath, Dave General Delivery, Forest Glen, Trinity County, Cal.

Musical Traditions 2375 Edgewater Terrace, Los Angeles, Cal. 90039

Neff, John (Rusty) 317 Pleasant St., Yellow Springs, Ohio 45387

Nicholas, General Custor and Sons Rt. 3, Carrollton, Ohio 44615

Peck, Elizabeth 932 Hilltop Mobile Home Ct., Ashville, N.C.

Presnell, Edd Box 235, Banner Elk, N.C. 28604

Proffitt, Frank Jr. Rt. 2, Todd, N.C. 28684

Reisler, Paul Rt. 1, Box 99, Keyser, W. Va.

Ritchie, Jean 7A Locust Ave., Port Washington, N.Y. 11050

Ritchie, Raymond 1404 Melvin St., Ypsilanti, Mich. 48197 (Sometimes will make a dulcimer. Write and see)

Rizetta, Sam See Rizetta String Instruments

Rizetta String Instruments 4616 So. 1st St., Arlington, Va. 22204

Sams, J. D. Sardis Rd., Euka, N.C.

Schilling, Jean and Lee P.O. Box No. 8, Cosby, Tenn. 37722

Seedpod Galiano Island, British Columbia, Canada

Shuttleworth, Don RR No. 3, Warren, Indiana 46792

Spence, Bill RD 1, Wormer Rd., Voorheesville, N.Y. 12186

Torstenson, Ray 301 So. Plymouth Rd., Huntsville, Ala. 35811

Tugel, Åke 266 Sea Cliff Ave., Sea Cliff, N.Y.

Vogel, Robert 2835 Alba Rd., Ben Lomond, Cal.

Wallo, Joseph International Bldg., Washington, D.C. 20004 (catalogue of guitar & dulcimer plans & materials, 954)

Ward, N.T. Jr. Vilas, N.C. 28692

Willcutt, J. Robert c/o Fred F. Moore Music Co., Lexington, Ky. 40502

Woehle und Söhne Hausmusikverlag, 6551 Waldböckelheim/über Bad Kreuznach, West Germany (this address for scheitholts only)

Wurtz, Howard P. 2503 Medcliff Rd., Santa Barbara, Cal. 93105

Young, Henry 153 W. Warren, Germantown, Ohio 45327

*Magic Mountain dulcimers are now made by Lyn Elder's former co-worker, and can be ordered from the J. C. Shellnutt Co., Rm. 232, Industrial Center Bldg., Gate 5 Rd., Sausalito, Cal.

Hammer Dulcimer Makers

No attempt has been made, in connection with the preparation of this book, to gather information about the makers and players of the hammer dulcimer, a psaltery-like instrument resembling a large shallow box strung with many strings (twenty-seven or more, usually), which are played by being struck with two wooden or felt "hammers," one in each hand of the player. This dulcimer has its origins in the Near Eastern countries, in and around Arabia and Turkey. In the United States, it was very popular with lumbermen in the North Woods in the 1800's, although it is found here and there throughout the country. The player whom I know best is Russell Fluharty. He can be found, more than likely, each August at the Fox Hollow Festival in Petersburg, New York, playing his hammer dulcimer on the little stage in the woods. He is president and founder of The Mountaineer Dulcimer Club, of Mannington, West Virginia, where he and his family live, and he and his grandson Jerry Taylor do public performances as *The Images*. Mr. Fluharty remembers old-timers saying that in the early part of the nineteenth century in the western part of Marion County, the hammer dulcimer was very popular, "even to the extent of being a status symbol in the home." Of his own beginnings as a player, he says, "When I was a young boy, Uncle Ezra would take me hunting and he kept telling me about the old dulcimer in his grain house loft. He gave it to me on the condition that if I would learn to play one tune, it would be mine. I learned, *Skip To My Lou*."

The following people make hammer dulcimers, although not all of them may want to make them for sale. Write a polite and friendly note, and you may find the hammer-dulcimer maker you have been looking for:

Campbell, J. Ralph Box 302, Mannington, W. Va. 26582

Dorogi, Dorogi Ellicott Rd., Brockton, N.Y. 14716

Gardner, Acel 213 Sanders Ave., Kingswood, W. Va. 26537

Gonzales, Joseph 529 Indian Hill Rd., Claremont, Cal. 91711

Rizetta, Sam 4616 So. First St., Arlington, Va. 22204

Wallace, William T. 863 Toulon Dr., Pacific Palisades, Cal. 42247

Epinette des Vosges Makers

Desaunay, Patrick 1 Rue do la Solidanté, 95 Argenteuil, France

Leroi-Gourh'an Christian and Michel Hindenoch 126 Ave. Philippe-Auguste, Paris 11e France

Maxson, Charles Volga, W. Va. 26238

*Minstrels do Gerardmer Epicerie Tabac de Gerardmer 80, France

Poussier, M. Grand Rue, Remirement 80, France

Richard, M. Fleury des Saint Loup, France

Rongier, Robert 2 Bis, Rue Albert 1er, 92 Asmères France

*Vancon, Jules le Crépiné, 88 Val d'Ajol France

Russ Flaharty and his grandson Jerry Taylor as they appear as the Images. The hammer dulcimer is 130 years old.

*Joelle feels that these are especially good ones.

Bibliography

Adler, Tom "How to Make an Appalachian Dulcimer, or, What to Do With Your Spare Time and Money." *Autoharp*, no. 30, Oct. 20, 1967. Reprinted in *Folknik,* vol. 4, no. 5, Sept. 1968

Apel, Willi *Harvard Dictionary of Music,* Second Edition. Harvard University Press, 1969. See, "Dulcimer."

Bailey, John *Making an Appalachian Dulcimer.* English Folk Dance and Song Society, London, 1966

Bay, Mel *Fun With The Dulcimer* Mel Bay Publications, Kirkwood, Mo., 1972

Bell, Corydon "The Fair at Gatlinburg." *Ford Times,* July, 1950

Bell, Red "Build a Dulcimer." *Stray Notes,* vol. 1, no. 6, Nov., 1965

Bishop, Elinor Hopper "Newcomer at Home in the Center of the Area Musical Activity." Foothill Life, Monrovia, Cal., May 7, 1966 Community Features section (Picture article about Hans Bender)

Boette, Marie *Singa Hipsy Doodle and Other Folk Songs of West Virginia,* The Junior League of Parkersburg, W. Va., 1971 P. XV (Introduction)

Brewer, Mary T. "A Golden Memory." *Mountain Life and Work,* vol. XL, no. 2, Berea, Ky., Summer, 1964

Bryan, Charles Faulkner "American Folk Instruments: The Appalachian Dulcimer." *Tenn. Folklore Soc. Bulletin,* vol. 18, no. 1, Mar., 1952 Also, June, 1952, and Sept., 1952
"The Appalachian Dulcimer Enigma." *Tenn. Folklore Soc. Bulletin,* vol. 20, no. 4, Dec., 1954

Burch, Gladys "Young Lady With a Dulcimer." *American Girl,* Aug., 1951

Burcham, Terry W. "Joe Gambill Dulcimer to Opryland." *Huntsville Assn. of Folk Musicians Newsletter,* no. 46, June 20, 1972
"Mountain Dulcimer." *Huntsville Assn. of Folk Musicians Newsletter,* no. 49, Sept. 20, 1972

Burrison, John "Biography of a Folk Singer." *Folkways Monthly,* Jan., 1963

Campbell, John C. *The Southern Highlander and His Homeland.* Russell Sage Foundation, N.Y. 1921, pp. 143-4

Clarke, Kenneth and Mary *A Concise Dictionary of Folklore.* Ky. Folklore Series No. 1, by *Ky. Folklore Record,* W. Ky. State College, Bowling Green, Ky., 1965

Combs, Jack "The Folk Singers of the Kentucky Highlands. . .A Trip to Hindman." *Spectrum,* vol. 1, no. 2, Spring, 1963

Combs, Josiah H. "The Highlander's Music." *Kentucky Folklore Record,* vol. 5, no. 4, Oct-Dec. 1959; first published in *Vient de Paraitre,* Paris 1926. Unused chapter of Dr. Combs' doctoral thesis, Sorbonne, 1925. Later included in the publication of the thesis as *Folk Songs of the Southern United States* American Folklore Society, Texas, 1967.

Creighton, Mildred Davidson "Jethro Amburgy: Dulcimer Maker." *Appalachian South,* vol. 1, no. 1, Summer, 1965

Davidson, Luckett "Learning Dulcimer is Kid Stuff. . ." *The Louisville Times,* Mar. 3, 1966 p. A34

Downs, Floyd and Mrs. Discussion under "Folklore," in the *Association for Childhood Education International Program,* 1950 Study Conference, Ashville, N.C., p. 32. Reprinted from *Souvenir Program, Craftsman's Fair of the Southern Highland, 1949*

Eaton, Allen W. *Handicrafts of the Southern Highlands.* Russell Sage Foundation, N.Y., 1937, pp. 199-204

English Folk Dance and Song Society Journal, vol. 2, 1935, "A Norwegian Player on the Langleik."

Evans, H. S. *How to Play the Mountain Dulcimer: A Manual for Beginners.* Lynchburg, Va., H. S. Evans, 1969

Gilfallan, Merrill C. "Dulcimers." *The Wonderful World of Ohio,* vol. 30, no. 1, Jan., 1966 (Dulcimer collection of Ann Grimes)

Glenn, Leonard "The Plucked Dulcimer of the Southern Appalachians." *Folkways Monthly,* vol. 1, no. 2, Jan., 1963

Griffin, Gerald "Transition in the Mountains." *The Courier-Journal Magazine,* Louisville, Ky., May 25, 1952

Guthrie, A. B. Jr. "Kentucky." *Holiday* magazine, Fifth Anniversary issue.

Haines, Aubrey B. "The John Jacob Niles Story." *Mature Years* (United Methodist Church magazine), March-May, 1972, Cokesbury Press, Nashville, Tenn.

Hamilton, Judith "The Mountain Dulcimer." *The Ozarks Mountaineer,* vol. 19, no. 2, Mar., 1971

Hammer, Philip L. "If You Like Mountain Music. . ." *Science and Mechanics,* vol. 35, no. 1, Jan., 1964

Hansen, Barbara "Sweet Dulcimer Sounds Rent Air in Southland." *Los Angeles Herald & Express,* April 27, 1961, p. D-2

Hart, Tim "The Appalachian Dulcimer." *Club Folk,* vol. 1, no. 5, July-Aug., 1968

Hastings, S. E., Jr. "Construction Techniques in an Old Appalachian Mountain Dulcimer." *Journal of American Folklore,* vol. 83, no. 330, Oct-Dec., 1970

Hickerson, Joseph C. *A Bibliography of Hammered and Plucked (Appalachian or Mountain) Dulcimers and Related Instruments.* Library of Congress, Music Division, Archive of Folk Song, Washington, D.C. 20540, Jan, 1973. Rev. from an earlier edition published in the *Journal of the Folklore Society of Greater Washington, vol. 3, nos. 1-2, Summer, 1972*

Hipkins, A. J. "Dulcimer." *Grove's Dictionary of Music and Musicians,* fifth edition, ed. by Eric Blom, London; Macmillan & Co. Ltd., vol. 5, pp. 799-800, 1954

Hoskins, R. Springer "Making Dulcimers is More Than a Hobby." (Story about A. L. Greynolds). *The Harlan Daily Enterprise,* Harlan, Ky. April 7, 196, p. 4

Irish Independent, Nov. 8, 1952, Dublin, Eire, "Of Ballads, Songs and Snatches. . ." p.5, signed with initials, I.M.

Jamison, Gladys V. "They Came Singing." *Mountain Life and Work,* vo. XXXIX, no. 2, Summer, 1963

Jeffreys, A. W. *Tuning and Playing the Appalachian Dulcimer.* Rev. ed., Appalachian Dulcimer Co., Staunton, Va., 1964

Lawless, Ray M. *Folksingers and Folksongs in America,* Duell, Sloan and Pearce, N.Y., 1960. Rev. ed., 1965. Chapter 9, "Folk Music Instruments."

Leach, Maria *Dictionary of Folklore Mythology and Legend,* Funk & Wagnalls Co., N.Y., 1949. See, "Dulcimer."

MacEachron, Len and Sue *Play the Dulcimer By Ear and Other Easy Ways,* Here, Inc., Minneapolis, Minn., 1970

McGill, Josephine "The Kentucky Mountain Dulcimer." *The Musician,* vol. 22, no. 1, Jan., 1917, p. 21

McSpadden, Lynn *Four and Twenty Songs for the Mountain Dulcimer.* Music transcribed by Dorothy French. The Dulcimer Shoppe, Mountain View, Ark., 1970

Brethren, We Have Met. Music transcribed by Dorothy French. The Dulcimer Shoppe, Mountain View, Ark., 1970

Marais, Joseph and Miranda *World Folk Songs.* Ballantine Books, New York, 1964, pp. 127-207

Marcuse, Sibyl *Musical Instruments: A Comprehensive Dictionary.* Doubleday & Co., Garden City, N.Y., 1964. See, "Appalachian Dulcimer," "Epinette," "Humle," "Hummel," "Langleik," "Scheitholt"

Mellon, Robert "Mountain Maestro of Hundon Falls." *Adirondack Life,* vol. 3, no. 1, Winter, 1972

Mercer, Henry C. "The Zithers of the Pennsylvania Germans." *A Collection of Papers Read Before the Bucks County Historical Society.* Vol. 5, 1926

Meyer, Carolyn "Handmade in America: The Delightful Mountain Dulcimer." *McCalls* magazine, vol. 98, no. 8, May, 1971

Mitchell, Howard W. *The Mountain Dulcimer-How To Make It and Play It—(After a Fashion).* Folk-Legacy Records, no. FS129, Sharon, Conn., 1966. Record and booklet, may be bought together or separately.

Mize, Robert "Dulcimers." *Foxfire* magazine, vol. 3, no. 1, Spring, 1969

Nicholson, Roger A. "The Appalachian Dulcimer." *Spin* magazine, Wallasey, Cheschire, England, vol. 5, no. 6, 1968; *Folknik,* San Francisco Folk Music Club newsletter, vol. 4, no. 5, Sept., 1968

Nonesuch for Dulcimer Scratchwood Music, 64 Dean St., London, England

Norlind, Tobias *Systematik der Saiteninstrumente.* Vol. 1, *Geschichte der Zither,* Musikhistorisches Muserm, Stockholm, 1936. See, "Trapezzither," and "Hummel."

Niles, John Jacob "Deft Hands Carve the Dulcimer." *Courier-Journal Magazine,* Jan. 20, 1952

Odell, Scott "The Appalachian Dulcimer." *1968 Festival of American Folklife* program booklet, Washington, D.C. Smithsonian Institution

Panum, Hortense *Langelegen: Som Danst Folkeinstrument.* Lehmann & State, Copenhagen, 1917. Two volumes.

Stringed Instruments of the Middle Ages. Translated by Jeffrey Pulver. Wm. Reeves, London, 1939; reprinted by Greenwood Press, Westport, Conn., 1970, and, Da Capo Press, N.Y., 1971. See, "The Scheitholt Family."

Pearse, John *Teach Yourself the Appalachian Dulcimer.* English Folk Dance and Song Society, London, 1966

The Dulcimer Book. A.T.V. Music; Welback Music, Ltd., London, 1970

Pearson, Candace "My Kind of Music." *Daily Pilot,* Riverside, Cal., April 3, 1972

Pickow, George "Dulcimer Maker," *Scenic South* Aug., 1955, p. 16

Pound, Louise *American Ballads and Songs*

Proffitt, Frank "Good Memories For Me" *Sing Out!* Vol. 15, no. 5, Nov., 1965

Promenade magazine, vol. 1, no. 7, Oct., 1940: "Musical Instruments of the American Folk."

Putnam, John F. "The Plucked Dulcimer." *Mountain Life and Work,* vol. 34, no. 4, 1958

The Plucked Dulcimer of the Southern Mountains Council of the Southern Mountains, Berea, Ky., 1957; rev. 1972

Ritchie, Jean *The Dulcimer Book.* Oak Publications, N.Y., 1963

Singing Family of the Cumberlands. Oxford U. Press, N.Y., 1955; reprinted by Oak Publications, N.Y., 1963

Russcol, Herb "Lonesome Ballits and Courtin' Songs." *Venture* magazine, July-Aug., 1969

Sorosi, Balint *Die Volksmusikinstrumente Ungarns.* VEB Deutscher Verlag fur Musik, Serie I, Band I, Leipzig, 1968

Schecter, Martha *Dulcimer Tuning.* M. Schecter, Rm. 14, N-211, M.I.T., Cambridge, Mass,, 1970

Seeger, Charles "The Appalachian Dulcimer." *Journal of American Folklore,* vol. 71, no. 279, Jan-Mar. 1958

Seeger, Peter "Johnny Appleseed, Jr.," column in *Sing Out!* magazine, vol. 9, no. 1, N.Y., Summer, 1959

Shoemaker, Henry W. *The Music and Musical Instruments of the Pennsylvania Mountaineers.* Times Tribune Co., Altoona, Pa., 1923

Smith, Ralph Lee "Some Pointers for Beginning Dulcimer Players." *Sing Out!,* vol. 20, no. 2, Nov-Dec., 1970

Snortheim, Olaf "Der Langeleik in Norwegian." *Pro Musica: Blatter fur Musik von Volk zu Volk,* no. 1, Jan-Feb., 1953

Stambler, Irwin, and Grelun Landon *Encyclopedia of Folk, Country and Western Music* St. Martins Press, N.Y., 1969 See, "Appalachian Dulcimer." Also, profiles of dulcimer players Paul Clayton, John Jacob Niles, Frank Proffitt, Jean Ritchie and Andrew Rowen Summers.

Steffens, Arlene "The Southern Highland Dulcimer and Its Craftsman." *Music Clubs Magazine,* vol. 49, no. 3, 1970

Stephens, Rockwell The Mountain Dulcimer." *Vermont Life,* vol. 24, no. 1, Autumn, 1969

Stradner, Fritz "Eine Alte Scheitholz-Zither." *Osterreichische Musikzeitchrift,* vol. 21, no. 9, Sept., 1966

"Vom Scheithol zur Kratz-Zither: Ein Beitrag zur Entwichlungsgeschechte der Zither." *Jahrbuch des Osterreishischen Volksliedwerkes,* vol. 18, 1969

Street, Julia Montgomery "Mountain Dulcimer." *North Carolina Folklore,* vol. 14, no. 2, Nov., 1966

Strickland, Sandy "Mastered Mountain Skill of Whittling." (Elizabeth Peck) Jacksonville Journal, Jan. 17, 1972

Sturgill, Virgil L. "The History of the Dulcimer." *Washington Folk Strums,* no. 1, April 1, 1964; no. 2, May 1, 1964

Talley, Rhea "Ambassador From Kentucky." *Courier-Journal Magazine,* Louisville, Ky.

Taylor, Vernon H. "From Fact to Fancy in Dulcimer Discoveries." *Tennessee Folklore Society Bulletin,* vol. 23, no. 4, Dec., 1957

Thomas, David "A Little Bit About the Appalachian Dulcimer." *Milwaukee Folk,* vol. 1, no. 3, 1972

Thomas, Jean, and Joseph A. Leeder *The Singin' Gatherin': Tunes From the Southern Appalachians.* Silver Burdett Co., N.Y. 1939
See, "Mountain Instruments and Their Usage," pp. 54-57

Tucker, George H. "A Love Ballad Needs a Dulcimore. . ." Norfolk *Virginia-Pilot,* June 22, 1969

Walin, Stig Die Schwedische Hummel: *Eine Instrumentenkindliche Untersuchung.* Nordiska Museet, Stockholm, 1952

Warner, Frank *Folk Songs and Ballads of the Eastern Seaboard: From a Collector's Notebook.* A lecture at Wesleyan College, Macon, Ga. Southern Press, Inc., 1963

Wilcox, Lee "You Can Make Sweet Music on the Appalachian Dulcimer." *House Beautiful,* vol. 104, no. 10, Oct., 1962

Wilhelm, Eugene J., Jr., and R. G. Carlson "Behind the Blue Ridge Song." *Mountain Life and Work,* vol. XLV, no. 4, April, 1969

Wilkie, Richard *Playing Lead Dulcimer.* Three City Press, 192 Mt. Hope Drive Albany, N.Y. 1972

Winters, Margaret *How to Play the Dulcimer.* Boston Music Co., Boston, 1963

Woehl, Waldemer *Kurze Spielanweisung fur das Scheitholz* Hausmusikverlag Soyen, Waldbockelheim, ub Bad Kreuznach, 1951
Die neuen Saiteninstrumente: Scheitholz und Psalterium (stapled mimeographed leaflets describing the instruments for sale), same address, 1960

Jean's great-grandfather Everidge's house, Hindman, Knott County, Kentucky. Still standing.

Discography

In these times of upsurging interest in the Appalachian dulcimer, it is impossible to have a complete discography, for new recordings are being made every day; some of the older ones are being dropped from catalogues; other old, discontinued ones are being brought up and reissued. The best thing I can think of to do here is to state which ones are, *as of now* available or unavailable*, but let the reader be warned that such a statement may change at any time. *Finding* the records is another matter, for, unless a record is on the charts, most ordinary record stores will not order it for you (many of my own friends have told me that their local store has assured them that one or another of my records or books was out of print, apparently to keep from having to order in small numbers). Some companies will sell to you direct, by mail. For those who may wish to try the different companies, addresses are given whenever possible. The Folkways address appears so often, that I have listed it only in connection with the first name on the list.

My purpose in including early, obscure, definitely unavailable (at present) records is to give as complete an historical picture as is possible of the capturing of the dulcimer sound; to assist serious collectors in their efforts to trace the old records; and, hopefully, to inspire the reissuance of more of the early recordings.

If new interest warrants future revisions of this book, we shall try to add the new recordings as they come along.

The performers are listed in alphabetical order, except that under the name heading for an individual or family having more than one record, these are listed as chronologically as possible. Dates of issue are given if they are known.

Individual Performers and Families

Armstrong, George and Gerry *Simple Gifts*. Dulcimer and guitar. Folkways FA 2335. 1961. Folkways Records, 43 W. 61st St. N.Y.C., N.Y. 10036 (a)

Bennett, Marjorie (Marty King) *Sing a Song of Childhood*. Dulcimer, autoharp, guitar, Irish harp. Judson Records, J-3028. (?)

Buckley, Bruce *Ohio Valley Ballads*. Guitar, dulcimer. Folkways, Fa 2025 (a)

Clayton, Paul *Cumberland Mountain Folksongs*. Dulcimer, guitar. Folkways, FA 1007. 1957 (a)

   Dulcimer Songs and Solos. Folkways, FA 2382 (a)

Fariña, Richard and Mimi *Celebrations For a Grey Day*. Dulcimer, guitar, autoharp. Vanguard, VRS 9174 (mono), and VSD 79174 (stereo). 1965 (a)

   Reflections In a Crystal Wind. Dulcimer, guitar, electric instruments. Vanguard, VSD 79204. 1965 (a)

   Memories. Dulcimer, guitar, various other instruments. Vanguard, VSD 79263. 1968 (a)

   The Best of Mimi and Richard Fariña. Dulcimer, guitar, various other instruments. Vanguard, VSD 21/22 (a)

Gainer, Dr. Patrick *Folk Songs of the Alleghenies*. Folk Heritage Records, DB 2122-3 (a) c/o Dr. Gainer, W. Va. University, Parkersburg, W. Va.

Greer, Mr. and Mrs. I. G. Recordings for the Paramount Co., New York, 1929. 78 rpm. No other information available on these recordings. (u)

   Library of Congress, Division of Music Recording, Record No. AAFS 34 of Album 7, *Anglo-American Ballads;* one song, "The Three Babes," with dulcimer by Mrs. Greer, 1941. Also, on Record No. AAFS 35, one song, "Sanford Barney," 1941; Album 12, Record No. AAFS 59, one song, "Sourwood Mountain," 1945; record No. AAFS 60, one song "Sweet William (Earl Brand)," 1946; Album 14, Record No. AAFS 69, "Old Smoky," 1945; Record No. AAFS 70, two songs, "Billy Grimes," "Common Bill," 1946. (a)

Grimes, Anne *Ohio State Ballads,* with dulcimer. Folkways FH 5217, 1957 (a)

Ledford, Homer *How to Play the Dulcimer* Instruction recording, 45 rpm. Order from Ledfords, 125 Sunset Heights, Winchester, Ky., 40391 (a)

   The Ledford Family (Songs We Love to Sing and Play),with Homer, Julia and Cindy. Order from Ledfords, address above.1972(a)

MacArthur, Margaret and Family *On the Mountains High,* with dulcimer, guitar, harp, dobro, banjo and fiddle. Living Folk Records, 65 Mt. Auburn St., Cambridge, Mass. 02138. 1971 (a)

*Code: (a) = available, (u) = unavailable, (?) = I don't know

Martin, Edsel *Edsel Martin Plays the Appalachian Dulcimer*. Vibrant Records, Route 2, Talbott, Tenn. (a)

Mitchell, Howard *Howie Mitchell*, with dulcimer. Folk-Legacy Records, Inc., Sharon, Conn. 06069. 1962 (a)

> *The Mountain Dulcimer: How to Make It and Play It (After a Fashion)*. Folk-Legacy Records, Inc. FSI-29 (Record and booklet may be bought separately). 1966 (a)

> *The Hammered Dulcimer: How to Make It and Play It* Folk-Legacy Records, Inc. FSI-43. 1972 (Included here because there is no separate discography for the hammer dulcimer) (a)

Moser, Artus *North Carolina Ballads*, with dulcimer and guitar. Folkways, FA 2112. 1955 (a)

Niles, John Jacob *The Seven Joys of Mary*, with dulcimer. Disc, 1946. No. 732, 78 rpm (u)

> *Early American Carols and Folk Songs,* with dulcimer. RCA Victor, M 718. Undated. 78 rpm (u)

> *American Folk and Gambling Songs,* with dulcimer. RCA Camden, CAL-219 (a)

> *American Folk Songs,* With dulcimer. RCA Camden, CAL-245 (a)

> *American Folk Love Songs,* with dulcimer. Boone-Tolliver, BTR-22 (?)

> *Ballads,* with dulcimer. Boone-Tolliver, BTR-23 (?)

> *I Wonder As I Wander,* with dulcimer. Tradition, TLP-1023. 1957 (a)

> *An Evening With John Jacob Niles,* with dulcimer. Tradition Recordings, TLP 1036 (a)

> *Fiftieth Anniversary Album,* with dulcimer. RCA Camden, CAL-330 (a)

Proffitt, Frank *Frank Proffitt Sings Folk Songs,* with dulcimer, banjo. Folkways Americana Series, 2360 (a)

> *Frank Proffitt Memorial Album,* with dulcimer, banjo. Folk-Legacy Records, Inc., Sharon, Conn. 06069 FSA-36. 1968 (a)

Ritchie, Edna *Edna Ritchie, Viper, Kentucky*, with dulcimer. Folk-Legacy Records, address above. FSA-3 (a)

*Ritchie, Jean *Jean Ritchie, Singing the Traditional Songs of Her Kentucky Mountain Family*. Dulcimer and guitar. Elektra-Stratford, N.Y. 10" lp, EKS-2.1952 (u)

> *Appalachian Mountain Songs*. Dulcimer and guitar. His Master's Voice, London, England; 2-record set of 78 rpm 10" discs, containing six songs. 1953 (?)

> *Songs From Kentucky.* Dulcimer and guitar. Elektra-Stratford, N.Y. 10" lp, EKL-25. 1954 (u)

> *Kentucky Mountain Songs.* Dulcimer and guitar. Elektra-Stratford, N.Y. 10" lp, EKL-25 1954 (u)

> *Courting Songs,* with Oscar Brand. Dulcimer and guitar. Elektra-Stratford, N.Y. 10" lp, EKL-22. 1954 (u)

> *Shivaree,* Jean Ritchie and Oscar Brand, with Tom Paley and Harry & Jeannie West. Dulcimer, guitar, banjo, mandolin. Esoteric Records, N.Y. 10" lp, ES-538. 1955 (u)

> *Jean Ritchie Field Trip.* Exchange of Kentucky songs with singers in Ireland, England and Scotland. Some dulcimer, guitar. Collector Limited Editions, CLE 1201. 1956. (u)

> *American Folk Tales and Songs.* Jean Ritchie and Paul Clayton, with Richard Chase telling mountain tales. Dulcimer and guitar. Tradition Records, TLP 1011 1956 (a)

> *Jean Ritchie At Home,* with sons Peter and Jonathan Pickow, and Alice Becker. Dulcimer, guitar, banjo, fiddle, recorder. Pacific Cascade Records, Vida, Oregon 97488 (a)

> *Saturday Night and Sunday Too.* Dulcimer and guitar, with occasional fiddle and banjo help. Riverside, RLP 12-620. 1956 (u)

> *Riddle Me This.* Jean Ritchie and Oscar Brand, with dulcimer, guitar, banjo. Riverside, RLP 12-646. 1957 (u)

> *Children's Songs and Games From the Southern Mountains.* Dulcimer, guitar, Folkways, FC 7054, 10" lp. 1957 (a)

> *Singing Family of the Cumberlands.* Readings from Jean Ritchie's autobiography of the same name (see bibliography), with dulcimer and guitar. Riverside, RLP 12-653. 1957 (u)

> *Songs From Kentucky.* (12" lp composite of the 2-record set of 10" lps from Argo, ARL 1011 and 1012). Westminster, N.Y., RG-17. 1957 (u)

> *The Ritchie Family of Kentucky.* Interviews with family members, with singing. Some dulcimer and guitar. Folkways, FA 2316. 1957 (a)

> *Courtin's a Pleasure* (12" lp composite of two 10" lps: EKL-22 by Jean Ritchie and Oscar Brand, and a 10" Tom Paley album). Elektra 122. 1957 (u)

> *Jean Ritchie* (12" lp composite of two 10" lps: EKL-22 by Jean Ritchie and Oscar Brand, and a 10" Tom Paley album). Elektra 122. 1957 (u)

> *Jean Ritchie, Oscar Brand and David Sear at Town Hall.* Dulcimer, guitar, banjo. Folkways, FA 2428. 1959 (a)

> *Carols of All Seasons.* Dulcimer, harpsichord, recorders. Tradition Records, N.Y., TLP 1031. 1959 (a)

> *Courting and Riddle Songs* (Reissue of Riverside, RLP 12-646, *Riddle Me This*). Washington Records, N.Y., WLP 706. 1959 (?)

> *British Traditional Ballads in the Southern Mountains.* Some dulcimer. Folkways, FA 2301 and FA 2302 (2-record set). 1961 (a)

> *Precious Memories.* Early "hillbilly" classics, with dulcimer, banjo, fiddle, parlor organ. Folkways, FA 2427. 1962 (a)

> *The Best of Jean Ritchie.* Dulcimer and guitar. Prestige International, FL 14009. 1962 (approx). (u)

> *The Appalachian Dulcimer.* Instruction record to accompany *The Dulcimer Book* (oak); record and book sold together or separately. Folkways, FI 8352 1963 (a)

> *Jean Ritchie and Doc Watson at Folk City.* Dulcimer, guitar, banjo and fiddle. Folkways, FA 2426. 1963 (a)

*All Jean Ritchie's available recordings may be ordered from Folklife Productions, 7A Locust Ave., Port Washington, N.Y. 11050.

Oscar Brand and Jean Ritchie (Reissue of Esoteric ES 538, *Shivaree*). Archive of Folk Music, Everest, FS 207. 1963 (approx). (?)

 A Time For Singing. Dulcimer, guitar, banjo, fiddle, bass, harmonica. Warner Brothers, WS 1592. 1965 (u)

 Clear Waters Remembered. Dulcimer, guitar, banjo, fiddle, bass. Sire Records, N.Y., SES 97014. Also issued in England by Transatlantic Records, XTRA 1123. 1970, N.Y. and 1971, England. (a) Sire Records, 165 W. 74th St., N.Y.C., N.Y. 10023

Ross, Claire and Pualine Hinchcliff *All In the Morning, Folk Carols of Britain and America.* Miss Ross plays dulcimer; Miss Hinchcliff, guitar. The Keepoint Recording Service, London, England, MF 12101. (?)

Simmons Family *Wandering Through the Rackensack.* Dulcimer, autoharp, and guitar. Rodney Peppenhorst Productions, P.O. Box 11211, Memphis, Tenn., 38111. Record No. V-3053 (a)

Smith, Ralph Lee *Allan Block and Ralph Lee Smith.* Dulcimer (Ralph's) fiddle and guitar. Meadowlands Records, 2301 Loring Place North, Bronx, New York 10468. Record No. MS-1 1972 (approx). (a)

 Dulcimer: Old Time and Traditional Music. Skyline Records, Rt. 1, Box 65F, Stephens City, Va. Record No. DD-102 (a)

Summers, Andrew Rowen *The Unquiet Grave.* Dulcimer accompaniment. Folkways, 10" lp, FA 2364. 1951 (a)

 The False Ladye. Dulcimer. Folkways, 10" lp, FA 2044. 1954 (a)

 The Lady Gay. Dulcimer. Folkways, 10" lp, FA 2041. 1954 (a)

 Christmas Carols. Dulcimer. Folkways, 10" lp, FA 2002. 1956 (a)

 Andrew Rowen Summers Sings (Ballads). Dulcimer, Folkways, 10" lp, FA 2348. 1957 (a)

 Seeds of Love. Dulcimer. Folkways, 10" lp, FA 2021. 1961 (a)

 Hymns and Carols. Dulcimer. Folkways, 10" lp, FA 2361. (a)

Winston, Nat T., Jr. *Learn to Play the Dulcimer.* Instruction record, 45 rpm. Don Sellers, Inc., Box 4185, Chattanooga, Tenn. 37405. 1969 (?)

Recordings of groups, such as festivals, record company samplers, school collections, etc., in which some dulcimer is used. Alphabetically, by title.

All Those People. . .Fox Hollow 1968 Vol. III. Jean Ritchie has one song with dulcimer. Fox Hollow Records, RD 1, Petersburg, N.Y. 12138 (a)

American Folk Song Festival. Aunt Dora Harmon has two songs with dulcimer on this recording of the 1958 festival in Ashland, Ky., organized by Jean Thomas, the Traipsin Woman. Folkways, FA 2358. (a)

American Folk Songs. Jean Ritchie sings eight songs with dulcimer on this Together-We-Sing series for lower grades, Follet Publishing Co., L-22 (a)

Anglo-American Songs and Ballads. Albums put out by the Library of Congress Music Division contains I. G. Greer singing to Mrs. Greer's dulcimer accompaniment; two songs on Album 7, two songs on Album 12, and three songs on Album 14. Recorded at various times between 1941 and 1946. (a)

Beech Mountain, North Carolina Vol. II. Viola Hicks plays four tunes on her dulcimer, accompanied by husband Captain Hicks on the guitar. Folk-Legacy Records, Sharon, Connecticut, 06069. 1965 (a)

Berkeley Farms—Country Music From Berkeley, California. Holly Tannen and friends play dulcimer and other instruments. Folkways, FA 2436. 1973 (a)

Folk Box, The. Jean Ritchie sings two songs, one with dulcimer. Elektra, in cooperation with Folkways, EKL-BOX. 1964 (?)

Folk Festival at Newport. Jean Ritchie, three songs with dulcimer; John Jacob Niles, one song with dulcimer. Vanguard, VRS 9064. 1959 (a)

Golden Ring. Howie Mitchell, George & Gerry Armstrong, and several other friends play dulcimers and other instruments, and sing. Folk-Legacy Records, Sharon, Conn. 06069. (a)

Instrumental Music of the Southern Appalachians. Mrs. Edd Presnell (Nettie) plays three tunes on her dulcimer. Tradition, TLP 1007. 1956 (a)

New Golden Ring-Five Days Singing. Whereas the original, *Golden Ring* (above) had nine members, the new one has twenty-six, and Lord knows how many dulcimer players, both Appalachian and hammer dulcimers. Folk-Legacy Records, address above. (a)

Pitter Poon, The Rain Come Doon— Vol. 1. 1967 Fox Hollow Festival. The Golden Ring sings two songs using dulcimer and other instruments. Fox Hollow Records, RD 1, Petersburg, N.Y. 12138 (a)

Pleasant and Delightful Vol. 1. Three songs using dulcimer: One by Rick and Lorraine Lee, one by John Cowles accompanied by Mary Rhodes, and the third by Joan Minkoff and Jeff Brewer. Living Folk Records, 65 Mt. Auburn St., Cambridge, Mass. 02138. 1971 (approx). (a)

Something to Sing About—Folk Singers Personal Choices, collected and arranged by Milt Okun. Record supplement to the book of the same name. Jean sings three songs with dulcimer. Macmillan, 1968 (a)

Sounds of History, The. Record supplement to the book *The Life History of the U.S.* Jean Ritchie sings with dulcimer, one song on Record 3, "The Growing Years." Time, Inc., 1963 (a)

Southern Mountain Folksongs and Ballads. Virgil L. Sturgill sings two songs with dulcimer, and Artus Moser sings four songs with dulcimer. Riverside, RLP 12-617 (u)

Traditional Music at Newport 1964, Part 2. Frank Proffitt sings one song with dulcimer and Jean Ritchie sings one song with dulcimer. Vanguard, VRS-9183 (a)

World Festival of Folk Song and Folk Dance, Biarritz-Pamplona, 1953. International Folk Music Council in cooperation with UNESCO. Jean Ritchie sings two songs with dulcimer. Westminster, WL 5334.